TEMPORARY EMPLOYMENT

Practice and Policy in Britain

BERNARD CASEY

Policy Studies Institute
in association with the Anglo-German Foundation

PSI Publications are obtainable from all good bookshops, or by visiting the Institute at: 100 Park Village East, London NW1 3SR (01-387 2171).

Sales Representation: Pinter Publishers Ltd.

Individual and Bookshop orders to: Marston Book Services Ltd, PO Box 87, Oxford, OX4 1LB.

A CIP catalogue record of this book is available from the British Library

PSI Research Report 678

ISBN 0 85374 352 5

Laserset by Policy Studies Institute
Printed by Bourne Offset Ltd., Iver, Bucks.

Contents

The tables for each chapter are to be found at the end of that chapter

Preface and acknowledgements

This book represents the British contribution to an Anglo-German study of temporary employment relationships conducted by Policy Studies Institute in this country and the Forschungsstelle Sozialökonomie der Arbeit of the Freie Universität Berlin, under the leadership of Michael Bolle, in Germany. The support of the Anglo-German Foundation for the Study of Industrial Society is gratefully acknowledged.

I should like to thank colleagues at PSI, namely Ian Christie, who contributed to the field work carried out for Chapter 5, Bill Daniel, the leader of the British project, and Michael White, who gave me encouragement and criticism throughout, Terence Hogarth, who provided computing assistance, Clare Pattinson, Karin Erskine and the word processing staff who typed many of the initial versions of the text. Thanks are also due to Pat Leighton, who explained the intricacies of employment law to me, the Manpower Services Commission and the Statistics Division of the Department of Employment, which produced the special tabulations from the Labour Force Survey used in the research, and all those representatives of management and trade unions who patiently explained their policies and practices to me.

Finally, I want to give special thanks to my wife Aline, herself a fixed term contract worker, to whom I dedicate this study.

1 What is a temporary worker?

Defining precisely the subject of this study - temporary work and temporary workers - is perhaps more complex than might first appear. The question posed by the title of this chapter can be answered by referring to the perception of the worker or the employer concerned and the views of the two parties will not always coincide. Moreover, temporary employment cannot be identified by reference to a specified period. In Britain, unlike certain other countries (for example, France), there is no maximum period specified in law which, if exceeded, makes an engagement permanent rather than temporary. Certain university researchers might be appointed on contracts with a duration of ten years. Are they temporary workers? Most 'fast food' chains, with a reputation - deserved or not - for hiring and firing, recruit staff on indefinite contracts of employment. Are their jobs temporary?

In this chapter we look at some of the definitions used in previous studies of temporary working and in some of the more important data sources available to us, and on this basis give some estimates of the number of persons who give could be regarded as temporary workers. We start by considering the definitions which individual workers give of their employment and then turn to employers' definitions, and thus focus more explicitly upon jobs than upon workers. We also show how employment protection legislation grants rights to workers dependent upon the duration of their employment, and how these rights can distinguish some temporary workers from other temporary workers or most temporary workers from many non-temporary workers. Finally, we outline the kinds of definition to be used in the rest of the study and give a brief outline of the direction it will take.

The perceptions of workers

Much of the quantitative information on temporary working currently available is generated through sources which rely on self-appraisal by members of the labour force themselves: samples of the population are asked if they are working and if they regard their work as temporary or permanent. The first substantial survey of the temporary labour force in Britain (Parker/Sirker, 1976), carried out for the public employment service by the Office of Population Censuses and Surveys (OPCS), considered as temporary workers both persons having a job that was available only for a limited period and persons regarding themselves as only temporarily available for the job which they were currently doing. The second component of the definition, however, is likely to have produced an over-reporting of the number of jobs in the economy which should be classified as temporary. A job could be permanent, but the person doing it might intend to occupy it for only a limited period of time, either because he was filling in until he found another job or because, for family, health or personal reasons, he was subsequently intending to take a break from work. In fact, less than half (48 per cent) of those who classified themselves as temporary workers in the OPCS study were in jobs which themselves were temporary - were available for only a finite period of time.

Self-appraisal forms the basis of classification in the most comprehensive and up-to-date survey containing information on temporary working, the OPCS/Department of Employment's Labour Force Survey (LFS), which is analysed extensively in Chapter 2. Respondents were required to classify their jobs as 'permanent' or 'temporary', but the same sort of 'over-counting' as occurred with the OPCS survey is possible. Rather than categorising their jobs, respondents might well have been describing their own attachment to it. The LFS shows that in Great Britain in 1984 there were some 1.5m persons who called themselves temporary workers. This was the equivalent of just over six per cent of the labour force, a share very similar to the seven per cent reported by the OPCS in 1976.

The perceptions of employers

We concentrate here specifically upon the jobs which members of the labour force are doing rather than upon the views they hold of their employment. Thus a temporary worker is one who is occupying a job which is available only on a temporary basis. In the literature on temporary working we were able to identify 11 categories of worker frequently referred to as persons occupying temporary jobs. We list and describe these in Overview 1 below.

Overview 1 Categories of temporary workers

1) *Consultants or freelancers* - who are normally self-employed and who move from organisation to organisation performing one-off or short duration tasks.

2) *Labour only sub-contractors* - who provide semi-skilled or skilled labour in the building industry.

3) *Casual workers* - who are brought in to undertake tasks of very short duration, who work at the request of an organisation but are not obliged to accept any offer of work and for whom the organisation has no obligation to provide work.

4) *Seasonal workers* - who are engaged to meet seasonal peaks in demand, particularly in such industries as distribution, tourism, agriculture and food processing.

5) *Fixed-term contract workers* - who are employed for a pre-determined period of time.

6) *Workers with a contract dischargeable by performance* - who are employed for the duration of a particular task.

7) *Workers on training contracts* - who are employed only for the duration of their training. These include apprentices and certain categories of trainee.

8) *Temporary workers on indefinite contracts* - who are employed to satisfy requirements for manpower which are recognised as temporary but the precise duration of which is uncertain, and who are informed in advance of their temporary status.

9) *Agency workers* - who are placed on a temporary basis by employment agencies with user organisations which themselves do not employ them but which pay the agency for their services.

10) *Employees of works contractors* - who are hired out by their direct employer to other organisations to undertake specific tasks, provide certain services or to replace absent employees.

11) *Participants in special programmes for the unemployed* - such as the Community Programme offering temporary jobs on 'socially useful' work projects, or the Youth Training Scheme, offering temporary training positions in enterprises.

Many of these categories, in fact, overlap each other. Thus labour only sub-contractors (2) can be viewed as a sub-category of freelancer (1) and certain workers on training contracts (7) as a sub-category of workers on performance contracts (6). Equally, seasonal workers (4) might be engaged on a casual basis (3), on fixed-term (5) or performance contracts(6), or even on open ended contracts (8). Participants in job creation programmes (11) are usually employed on fixed-term contracts (5), whilst those in special training schemes (11) *might* be considered as a form of worker on a training contract (7). Some consultants and freelancers (1) market their services via an agency (9), and some employees of works contractors (10) closely resemble agency workers (9).

To date there has been only one attempt to assess the number of temporary jobs in Great Britain, that undertaken by the Institute of Manpower Studies (IMS) in 1984 (see Meager, 1985). Since the terms that can be used to describe temporary workers are highly fluid and subjective, the IMS had to construct its own broad definition, and it did so by adapting a definition initially proposed by the Federation of Personnel Services, the body representing private recruitment and employment agencies (see FPS, 1983). The IMS asked employers about the number of persons they were currently engaging whose employment with the organisation was recognised by both sides to be on a temporary basis, irrespective of whether the individuals were its employees. The results of their small survey suggested that rather over seven per cent of all jobs were temporary jobs. However, there are two reasons for being sceptical of this finding. First, it is by no means certain that the sample of employers questioned was representative; second, employers using temporary workers may have been more likely to respond to such an inquiry than those which did not. As a consequence, the IMS may have overestimated the number of temporary jobs in the economy.

The distinctions in labour law

Although labour law does not make any general references to temporary workers, they can sometimes be distinguished by the degree of security which they enjoy in their jobs. This is because employment protection legislation (The Employment Protection (Consolidation) Act, 1978) bases many of the rights it accords to workers on the length of their service with their employer. This in turn means that some of these rights are not enjoyed by those whose employment lasts only a short while. On top of this, certain categories of temporary worker are explicitly excluded from particular rights, and others are excluded from any rights at all.

Length of service is not the only factor determining the degree of coverage by protective legislation. Two other factors also intervene. First, workers acquire employment rights only if they have the status of being 'dependent employees'. However, the distinction in employment law between a 'dependent employee' and a 'self-employed' worker is not always clear (see Leighton, 1983; Davies/Friedland, 1984). It is certainly not the case that the joint decision of the contracting parties to label the relationship as being one or the other suffices. Nor is it sufficient that a worker pays income tax and makes social security (National Insurance) contributions at the rates applicable to a dependent employee (even when his 'employer' deducts these at source) for him to be categorised as being under a contract of employment. What to the layman appears to be a situation governed by a contract of employment can be one which the courts would define as self-employment, governed by a contract to provide services or by a special 'contract of its own kind'.

Indeed, of the 11 commonly referred to categories of temporary workers described in the previous section, four will generally be treated as self-employed for labour law purposes - namely consultants or freelancers, labour only sub-contractors, casual workers and agency workers. Fixed-term contract workers, workers on contracts dischargeable by performance, employees of works contractors and temporary workers on indefinite contracts will normally be treated as dependent employees; so too will seasonal workers who are not simultaneously casual workers. Some workers on training contracts have employee status, but the large majority of participants in the special labour market programme for training young persons (the Youth Training Scheme), together with certain so called 'cadets', are not employees and instead have a special status of 'trainee'. The position of agency workers and casual workers (and of certain trainees) is anomalous in that they are usually treated as employees for tax and social security law purposes. Most of them are liable to make payments and contributions in the same manner as and at the rates applicable to dependent employees, and most people other than experts in labour law would regard them as dependent employees[1]. The labour law position of agency and casual workers is discussed further in Chapters 5 and 6 respectively.

Second, labour law makes most rights dependent upon the worker concerned normally being employed for at least 16 hours per week or, if they have had at least five years continuous service, between eight and 16 hours per week[2]. Here the principal exceptions concern rights to ante-natal leave and to protection against victimisation or dismissal for trade union activities. Each of these rights is independent of the worker's length of service.

The most important of the service-related rights (for more details see IDS, 1985 and *ibid*, 1986a) are those becoming operative after four weeks, and after two years of service. Employees with at least four weeks service are entitled to a minimum period of notice (one week, increasing after two years by an additional week for each additional year of service) and to pay in case of layoffs caused by shortages of work (up to a maximum of five days per calendar quarter). Employees with at least two years service are entitled to statutory compensation is made redundant, the level of such compensation depending upon age and service (one and a half weeks pay for each year of employment from the age of 41, one weeks pay for each year from the age of 40 to 22 and half a weeks pay for each year from 18 to 21, with a maximum of 20 years reckonable service). They are also protected against 'unfair' dismissal (dismissal without good cause) and can be awarded compensation or reinstatement if their case is shown to be proved. Unfair dismissal legislation has been the subject of considerable political controversy in recent years. With the intention of reducing 'barriers to recruitment', the government has raised in two steps the qualifying period from the six months that applied until 1979 to one year and then to two years[3].

With rights to notice, protection from unfair dismissal and redundancy compensation, certain exclusions apply to some temporary workers. Thus, no notice of dismissal has to be given to workers on fixed-term or performance contracts when their contracts are due to expire, since they have received this notice at the start of their employment[4]. The non-renewal of a fixed-term contract can (not must) constitute an unfair dismissal, but where contracts are due to last more than a year employers are entitled to insert clauses according to which the worker waives his rights to contest a non-renewal. Equally, where the fixed-term contract is to last for at least two years, rights to redundancy compensation can be waived. Finally, employees on performance contracts can claim neither unfair dismissal nor redundancy compensation on the expiry of their contracts, since in law there has been no dismissal. Rather, the purpose of the contract has ceased to exist.

Service with the employer has to be continuous for the employee to benefit from each of the above described rights, but there are certain interruptions of employment time which are not regarded as breaking continuity (see IDS, 1985). These are mainly breaks consequent upon a 'temporary cessation of work'. Thus a college teacher employed on a series of fixed-term contracts, each for the duration of the teaching year but not covering the long vacation, was able to claim continuity because these vacations could be described as temporary cessations of work. Nevertheless, for a cessation to be regarded as 'temporary', it has to be of short duration relative to the spells of employment around it. Much seasonal working, for example in hotels over summer time or in agriculture during harvest time, is likely to involve breaks in employment too long to be considered temporary. Continuity might be also maintained if an arrangement for re-engagement at some future date or a request to remain available for work is made before the date of commencement of a period of non-working. This holds regardless of the length of the period of non-working. On the other hand, the fact that a particular person is customarily re-hired at the end of that period is not normally sufficient to establish continuity.

Using the LFS data we have been able to make some broad estimates of the extent to which members of the labour force are covered by the various employment protection provisions outlined above. These are shown in Table 1.1, in which those who classify themselves as 'temporary' are also distinguished. The approximate nature of these estimates must be stressed. The LFS's definition of self-employment reflects tax and social security rather than labour law definitions, and casual workers and agency workers are therefore likely to be miscounted. Categories such as trainees have been counted in the dependent labour force despite the fact that they do not enjoy any employment protection rights, and those temporary workers for whom special exclusions apply cannot be separately identified. Not all relevant lengths of service (notably four weeks) are distinguishable, although we were able to give some indication of the impact of raising the qualifying period for protection against unfair dismissal.

A rather smaller proportion of the temporary than of the total labour force is covered by provisions, such as protection from dismissal because of trade union activities, which require no minimum service or hours. This is largely because a greater proportion of temporary workers are self-employed. Whilst some 80 per cent of the total labour force is likely to be entitled to at least a minimum notice period of one week, the same applies to well under 60 per cent of the temporary labour force. This is explained by a higher share of the latter working part-time. Finally, although some 60 per cent of the total labour force enjoys protection from unfair dismissal and rights to compensation in case of redundancy, under 10 per cent of the temporary labour force has this protection. The extension of the qualifying period from six months to one year and then to two years had a potentially greater impact upon the temporary than on the total labour force. Some one fifth of temporary workers were excluded from resort to the law's provisions, compared to one eighth of the total labour force.

Conclusions

We have outlined some of the difficulties in defining what is meant by a temporary worker and suggested that there is no single definition which can be used. The extent of a worker's commitment to his job is of some importance. Some workers will treat their jobs as temporary even if these jobs are themselves of an indefinite duration. On the other hand, regardless of the availability of the individual worker, there are certain jobs which are available only for a limited period. Certain workers are entitled to the full range of provisions established by employment protection legislation, and yet their jobs might be considered by their employers as temporary. Others have not yet achieved more than minimum coverage, even though their jobs are considered as of indefinite duration.

In the rest of this book we adopt a pragmatic approach, relying upon such definitions as are available for each of the aspects of temporary working studied. In Chapter 2 (which contains the bulk of our analysis of the LFS) we look at the occupations and characteristics of those persons who describe themselves as temporary workers, regardless of the nature of their jobs. Chapter 3 has the results of an establishment survey (the PSI/DE/ESRC/ACAS Workplace Industrial Relations Survey) covering employers' use of two specific forms of temporary worker - those on fixed-term contracts and those provided by an agency - and is concerned with temporary jobs rather than temporary workers. In Chapter 4, where we examine the relationship between temporary working and unemployment using the LFS and in particular the PSI's Unemployed Flow Survey, we also make reference to the nature of jobs themselves. Chapters 5-7 (based upon case studies undertaken in some 30 employing organisations) describe the kinds of circumstances where temporary workers are used, the kind of jobs the temporary workers do, who the temporary workers are and the extent to which they are available for work on other than a temporary basis. We also discuss in more detail the situation of certain categories of temporary workers in labour law, with the object of discovering the adequacy of current provisions and the efficacy of any reforms. Chapter 5 looks at agency working, Chapter 6 at casual working and Chapter 7 at short-term contract working involving both fixed-term and open-ended employment contracts. The final chapter (Chapter 8) summarises the findings.

Notes

1. Certain trainees, particularly those on special youth training measures, are in receipt of grants/allowances rather than wages and pay neither tax nor social insurance contributions.

2. In a recent White Paper the government proposed raising the threshold of these hours to 20 and 12 hours respectively (see Secretary of State, 1986).

3. Whether unfair dismissal legislation did have the negative consequences suggested for it is open to question. A number of enterprise surveys (for example, Daniel/Stilgoe, 1978; Clifton/Tatton Brown, 1979; Evans/Goodman/Hargreaves, 1985) suggest its impact to have been negligible, whilst the results of econometric analyses have proved inconclusive (for example, Nickel, 1982).

4. However, employers cannot evade notice requirements by using a series of fixed-term contracts of less than four weeks, since a person continuously employed on such contracts for three months or more will be treated as if he were on an indefinite contract.

Table 1.1   Proportion of labour force covered by employment protection legislation

Percentages

	All workers	Temporary workers
excluded because self-employed	11	15
covered by provisions requiring		
- no minimum hours of work service	89 (86)	85 (60)
- minimum hours but no service	82 (79)	57 (52)
- minimum hours and 6 months service	75 (72)	31 (28)
- minimum hours and 1 year service	68 (66)	14 (12)
- minimum hours and 2 years service	61 (59)	9 (8)

Figures in brackets show proportions if proposals to raise qualifying hours to 12 and 20 per week were given effect.

Source: 1984 LFS

2 The temporary workforce: findings from the Labour Force Survey

The Labour Force Survey (LFS), which is based on a half per cent sample, collects information from about 80,000 households and about 120,000 people each year. At the level at which most analysis is conducted in this chapter, cell sizes are sufficiently large for the results reported to be considered statistically significant. The fact that a relatively high proportion (nearly 40 per cent) of responses are 'proxy' responses (not the responses of the individual concerned but of another member of the household, often a spouse) has suggested that LFS data should be interpreted with some caution. However, one attempt to test the extent of misreporting (Martin/Butcher, 1982) found that, in general, it was not so great as to be a cause for concern. Where we have specific reservations we mention them in the text. Because it is conducted at a particular point in the year, the spring, the LFS cannot be used to investigate seasonal variations in the size or structure of the temporary workforce. Nor can it be used to quantify fully the number of temporary jobs in the economy. As we made clear in the previous chapter, its definition of temporary workers might well include people whose jobs are available on other than a temporary basis, but who only intend to stay in these jobs for a limited period of time. Nevertheless, it does provide the most extensive summary of the temporary workforce available.

In this chapter we use the LFS to look at the industrial and occupational distribution of temporary working. We consider some of the forms this can take, distinguishing seasonal, temporary or casual working from fixed contract working, self-employed and agency supplied temporary workers from those who are directly employed, and full-time temporary workers from part-time temporary workers. We also use the survey to examine the significance of small establishments as employers of temporary workers and the regional distribution of temporary employment, to give the personal characteristics of temporary workers - concentrating on their sex, age and marital status - and to discuss some of the reasons given by temporary workers for working on this basis. Where the LFS gives details of other characteristics explaining why people might define themselves as temporary workers, particularly being a participant in a special employment programme, we also make reference to them. Finally, we compare the findings of the 1984 survey with those of the 1983 and 1986 surveys to see if there has been any growth in temporary working over this period.

Industrial and occupational distribution
An overview of the industrial distribution of the temporary workforce is given in Table 2.1. In 1984 just over six per cent of all workers, or some 1.5m people, regarded their jobs as temporary. Quite substantial differences are to be observed depending on industrial sector. Whilst in manufacturing industry the proportion of the workforce which is temporary stands at only just over three per cent, in the service sector it stands at well over seven per cent. Moreover, it is particularly within two broad areas of services - distribution, hotels and catering, and 'other services' - that temporary workers are to be found. Together they account for nearly two-thirds of the entire temporary labour force but rather under half of total employment. Table 2.1 gives additional information about these two broad industrial areas, showing that it is in the retail trade and the hotels and catering industry in the first of these, and public administration, education, medical services, 'other services to the public', recreational and cultural services and personal services in the second, where the proportion of temporary workers is greatest and/or where an important share of the temporary workforce is to be found.

13

ional distribution of temporary workers, shown in Table
the industrial divide portrayed in the preceding paragraph.
trial occupations generally have a lower share of temporary
wor... .an do service occupations. This seems to obtain even when
occupational levels are taken into account, so that temporary working
is more prevalent amongst people in higher level service occupations
than amongst those in higher level industrial occupations. However,
the lower the level of the occupation, the higher the proportion of the
workforce working on a temporary basis. Both of these findings are in
line with what human capital theory predicts. According to that theory,
temporary working is likely to be more prevalent in occupations where
skills are general rather than specific and in occupations where little or
no training is required. A more detailed examination of occupations
confirms these points.

There is a relatively high incidence of temporary working amongst
professionals in education (particularly school and university teachers
and researchers), who have highly transferable skills, and amongst
professionals in health and welfare (doctors and nurses), for whom the
same holds. The large number of temporary clerks and secretaries is
also a function of the generality of their skills. The large share of 'other'
personal service and 'other' operatives working on a temporary basis
is explained by the fact that they are in jobs for which little training is
necessary. Equally, the low level of temporary working by managers
and administrators, by supervisors and by engineering craftsmen is a
function of the high level of specific training that their jobs usually
entail.

Forms of temporary working
The LFS distinguishes between temporary workers who describe
themselves as having 'seasonal, temporary or casual jobs' and those
with 'jobs done under contract or for a fixed period of time'.
Unfortunately these two categories overlap[1], whilst those temporary
workers (or those who are giving proxy answers for them) who are
unsure of the precise nature of their temporary employment are also
more likely to describe themselves as falling into the first category. We
would expect temporary workers employed on open-ended contracts to
do so as well.

Some two-thirds of all temporary workers regard themselves as having seasonal, temporary or casual jobs and only one third as having fixed contract jobs, but with substantial differences between industries and occupations. An industry breakdown, which is given in Table 2.3, shows that in 'other manufacturing' (particularly the food and drink industry and printing) the share of temporaries working on a seasonal, temporary or casual basis is even higher (some 80 per cent). In the remaining branches of manufacturing and production, however, the share is much lower, and it is here that fixed contracts are the most important means of engaging temporary labour. Within the distribution, hotels and catering sector it is, again, seasonal, temporary or casual working which predominates, but within the 'other services' sector the picture is more varied. Thus, within public administration, health and particularly the research industry, fixed contracts are the norm, and they are also relatively more important in education. In personal services and domestic services, on the other hand, there is a predominance of casual, temporary or seasonal type relationships for temporary workers.

These patterns are reflected in the occupational data. As Table 2.4 shows, the proportion of seasonal, temporary and casual workers is generally higher amongst persons in service occupations than amongst persons in industrial occupations, but also the proportion of fixed contract workers is higher the more skilled the level of occupation. Temporarily employed engineers and scientists and technicians are mainly engaged upon fixed contracts, as are skilled operatives and craftsmen (other than in construction). Semi and unskilled operatives are mainly engaged upon a seasonal, temporary or casual basis. Sales workers and lower grade personal service workers are also largely employed in this fashion. In all of these instances the term 'seasonal' or 'casual' is probably a better description of their status. However, the relatively high (if lower than average) proportion of people in the educational and health occupations regarding themselves as in the seasonal, temporary or casual category might result from many of them being engaged on a 'temporary' basis but for an unspecified (non-fixed) period, perhaps to replace workers who are absent or until regular or permanent recruitments can be made. The same argument probably also applies to clerical and secretarial occupations, where again the seasonal, temporary or casual relationship predominates.

Temporary workers can be differentiated according to whether (at least in the layman's eyes) they are directly employed, self-employed or the employee of a third party such as an agency. People who work through and are paid by agencies numbered only some 50,000 in 1984 and made up only just over three per cent of the total temporary labour force. Nearly half the agency workers are working in the banking, finance and business services sector, although this might be a consequence of that sector being the one in which employment agencies/business are located, and another fifth are in 'other services', of which half are in medical and health services. More significant is the fact that they are concentrated in a limited number of types of job. As Table 2.5 shows, some 70 per cent of agency workers are in eight narrowly defined occupations - systems analysts and programmers, nurses, draughtsmen, clerks, secretaries and receptionists, office machine operators, telephonists, and bus and lorry drivers - which account for only 18 per cent of total employment[2]. The single occupational group of secretaries and receptionists itself accounts for nearly one in four of all such workers. Interestingly, in none of the eight occupations in the share of temporary workers is particularly high - it is around or only slightly above the average in each case. Rather, it is the share of temporary workers who work via and are paid by an agency which is many times higher than average. In other words, agencies have captured a substantial share of the temporary employment market in these occupations.

As we have already seen in Chapter 1, the proportion of the temporary labour force who consider themselves self-employed (15 per cent) is rather higher than that of the workforce as a whole (11 per cent). A considerable proportion of self-employed temporary workers are to be found in industries in which the overall level of self-employment is high. As Table 2.6 shows, rather over one fifth came from the construction industry, a similar proportion from the recreational industry, personal services and domestic services together, and a further 10 per cent from business services. However, in the distribution, hotels and catering industry the picture is rather different. Instead of being as high or even higher than the overall rate of self-employment, the rate of self-employment amongst temporary workers is only half that for all workers. Although the tendency for a substantial share of the self-employed to classify themselves as 'managers' (see Creigh et al, 1986) reduces the meaningfulness of occupation analysis, the general picture is one of a higher share of self-employment amongst temporary workers who could be viewed as 'professionals' and a much lower level amongst those in low grade white collar jobs. Nevertheless, semi and unskilled operatives constitute one in eight of all self-employed temporaries and that persons with low grade personal service occupations constitute a further one in ten.

A substantial proportion of the temporary labour force works on a part-time basis. Whilst just over one fifth (21 per cent) of the total labour force have part-time jobs, over a half (54 per cent) of the temporary labour force are part-timers. In certain industries the proportion is even higher. Thus in retail distribution and catering it reaches 80 per cent, in domestic services 90 per cent. Equally, the proportion of temporary workers in sales and lower grade personal service occupations with part-time jobs is high (81 and 85 per cent respectively). Amongst those in more skilled occupations, as might be expected, it is much lower. Thus for technicians and draughtsmen it is only 11 per cent. However, amongst education professionals (primarily teachers) the proportion stands as high as 66 per cent, perhaps reflecting the practice of certain local authorities of employing all part-time teachers on a temporary basis (see NUT, 1983). Table 2.7 presents further details of part-time temporary working.

The overlap between temporary and part-time working is most pronounced with respect to seasonal, temporary and casual working. Nearly 70 per cent of seasonal, temporary or casual workers are also part-timers compared to only a quarter of fixed contract workers. Occupations with a high part-timer share are also those with a high casual worker share, and there are grounds for thinking that in certain cases the two categories of worker are functional equivalents. Both are likely to involve low hours of work, the absence of any formal documentation of the employment relationship (for example a contract of employment), and earnings below the tax and social insurance

17

thresholds. This overlap would explain the apparent confusion of the terms 'temporary' and 'part-time' under survey respondents noted by some previous commentators (Newton/Parker, 1975). For at least some categories of worker the terms are, synonymous.

The way in which temporary working overlaps with each of the other forms of 'non-standard' working identifiable through the LFS - namely self-employment and part-time working - is shown in Diagram 1. As can be seen, it is not only that some temporary workers are self-employed and some are part-timers; a sizeable minority are both. Attempts to disaggregate the growth of 'non-standard' employment are likely to be rendered more difficult by an inability to determine whether it is the 'temporariness', the 'self-employedness' or the 'part-timeness' of any particular employment which is its predominant characteristic.

Diagram 1   Overlaps between various forms of 'non-standard' worker

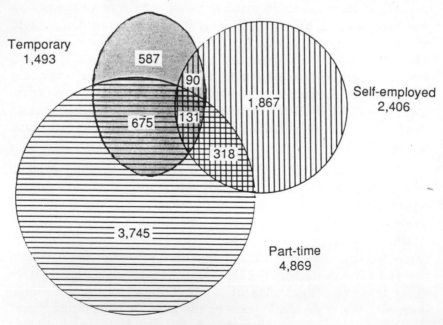

Source: own calculations from 1984 LFS

Location

A further way of looking at how temporary workers are engaged is to consider the size of the establishment in which they work. The LFS allows us to identify separately those who work in establishments with a labour force of not more than 25 people. Again we find an over-representation of temporary workers in the small establishments sector: some 50 per cent are employed there compared to 37 per cent of all workers. In general this appears to be a function of the kind of sectors in which they are working, or of the kinds of occupations which they have. Thus, small establishments in retailing and in hotels and catering do not appear to make much more use of temporaries than do larger establishments[3].

The regional distribution of temporary workers followed the distribution of total employment fairly closely and as such does not deserve any special attention. However, the small sub-category of agency workers prove to be concentrated heavily in the South East region. Whilst one third of the total labour force reside there, just over seven-tenths (72 per cent) of all agency workers do so. To a large extent this reflects the occupational distribution of the agency worker labour force and the particular characteristics of the clerical/secretarial labour market in that part of the country [see in more detail, Chapter 5].

Personal characteristics

The majority of the temporary workforce are women. They account for 41 per cent of the entire labour force, but 54 per cent of the temporary labour force. They are also disproportionately represented amongst a particular category of temporary workers, namely those working on a seasonal, temporary or casual basis, where they make up 64 per cent of the total, and amongst agency workers, where they account for 63 per cent of the total. Fixed contract workers, on the other hand, are predominantly men: women account for only 37 per cent. As Table 2.8 shows these results can largely be explained by the occupational distribution of temporary working. Nevertheless, in certain occupations there was still a tendency for women to be over-represented amongst those working on a temporary basis. This was particularly so with the education professions and with low skilled industrial jobs where women made up 57 per cent and 23 per cent respectively of the total workforce but 79 per cent and 32 per cent respectively of the temporary workforce.

The concentration of women in industries and occupations where seasonal, temporary and casual rather than fixed contract working prevails also goes much of the way to explaining why the majority of female temporary workers are also part-timers. Whilst 44 per cent of all women work part-time, 70 per cent of temporary women and 79 per cent of the sub-category of seasonal, temporary and casual women do so. More remarkable in some ways is the overlap between part-time working and temporary working among men. Only four per cent of all men work part-time, but 35 per cent of all temporary men do so. Indeed, of the category of 'male part-timers', 40 per cent are accounted for by men with temporary jobs, of whom the large majority (78 per cent) are in seasonal, temporary or casual jobs.

Temporary workers, as Table 2.9 shows, are considerably younger than the generality of workers. Well over a quarter are aged under 20 years, of whom nearly 30 per cent are still at school[4], and nearly a quarter of all those in the labour force who are under 20 are working on a temporary basis. Amongst over 20 year olds the share of temporary workers is below the average, and it falls for each age group until the pensionable age is reached. An increased share of temporary workers does, however, become apparent for women over the age of 60 and men over the age of 65.

Reasons for taking temporary jobs

The LFS asks questions about reasons for taking a temporary job, offering four responses: 'because the contract included a period of training', 'because a permanent job could not be found', 'because a permanent job was not wanted' and 'other/no reason'. As Table 2.10 shows, the single most important reason for taking a temporary job was that a permanent job was not available, although even then this was the reason given by only one third of all temporary workers. However, as the table also shows, there were substantial differences between men and women. More than four out of ten men gave this as their reason for taking temporary work and only 16 per cent claimed they did not want a permanent job. On the other hand, for women not wanting a permanent job was the single most important reason given, and a considerably smaller share said they were working on a temporary basis because permanent work was not available. For married women this tendency was even more pronounced. Temporary workers working part-time were also more likely to have taken temporary jobs because they did not want permanent jobs, whilst among those working full-time inability to find a permanent job was by far the most frequent reason given. Reflecting these last results is the finding that fixed-contract workers tended to have taken their temporary jobs in response to a lack of permanent work, whilst seasonal, temporary or casual workers had done so because they did not want permanent work. Agency workers, too, were more likely to give not wanting a permanent job as their reason for working on a temporary basis. Finally, only a minority of self-employed temporaries would actually have preferred a permanent job. Most gave 'other reasons' as their response.

Age strongly relates to the reason for taking temporary work. As Table 2.10 shows, only a minority of all temporary workers said that having a training contract was their reason for having taken a temporary job. It was of greater significance for young persons: under 25 year olds accounted for 84 per cent of all those working on a temporary basis for this reason. On the other hand, it should be noted that even for 20-25 year old temporary workers, by whom it was stated most frequently, this reason was not of great importance - it was put forward by only 15 per cent of them. Table 2.11 shows that inability to find a permanent job remained the most frequent reason given by young people for taking temporary work. For people over pension age on the other hand, not wanting a permanent job was the most common reason. Moreover, almost all (82 per cent) temporary workers age 60 and over considered themselves retired and nearly all (93 per cent) of these were working part-time.

Of those temporary workers who did not want a permanent job, nearly half (47 per cent) had been economically inactive one year previously, and less than two per cent had been unemployed. Many of the first group, it can be presumed, were married women, while some were teenagers who had taken part-time temporary jobs whilst still at school. Equally, nearly half (47 per cent) of those who had taken temporary jobs because these provided a source of training had entered the labour market only in the past 12 months. Many of these were young people.

As well as the reasons given in answer to direct questions, the LFS provides information on the importance of a further reason for taking a temporary job - that of being a participant in a special employment programme. Indeed, as Table 2.12 shows, some 13 per cent of all temporary workers are also participants in special employment measures. Participants in the Youth Training Scheme (YTS) make up the largest share of these, accounting for nearly nine per cent of all temporary workers, and participants in the Community Programme (CP) together with a small number in the Community Industry programme make up almost all the remainder, accounting for just over four per cent. Most participants in special programmes simultaneously answered that they were in temporary jobs because they had been unable to find permanent work; a small proportion, consisting mainly of YTS participants, saw their places on the scheme as jobs which were temporary because they involved a contract for training.

Amongst teenagers in temporary jobs the importance of special measures was particularly pronounced. Some 32 per cent of all temporary workers in this age group were participating in special measures, almost all (29 per cent) in the YTS. Of the 20-25 year olds in temporary jobs 14 per cent were in special measures, and most of these (nearly 12 per cent) were in the CP. Finally, the extreme over-representation of teenagers amongst temporary workers, pointed out earlier, can be put into perspective. Nearly a third of under 20 year old temporary workers were temporary workers because they were participants in special employment measures, and 29 per cent were still at school.

Changes over time

The proportion of participants in special employment programmes amongst temporary workers has to be taken into account in assessing the growth of temporary working over time[5]. The LFS has asked the same question about temporary working only since 1983[6] and the latest survey results available are those from 1986. Over these years the size of special employment programmes increased substantially, largely as a consequence of a tripling of the number of places on the Community Programme. If special programme participants are subtracted from the temporary labour force we find that, whilst it grew between 1983 and 1986, it did so only very slightly - by only just over five per cent. This is shown in Table 2.13. However, it is also necessary to take account of the growth of total employment, again excluding special programme participants, over the years in question. As a proportion of the total labour force, the temporary labour force remained virtually constant at 5.5 to 5.6 per cent between 1983 and 1986. The claims of those commentators (for example Meager, 1985; LRD, 1987) who suggest there has been a growth in temporary working in recent years are given no support whatsoever by these results[7]. Since the period in question has been one of economic growth, and since it is argued that the demand for temporary workers grows faster than the demand for labour as a whole in periods of rising economic activity[8], our findings are particularly noteworthy.

Conclusions
On the basis of self-classification, just over six per cent of the labour force in Britain in 1984 could be described as having temporary jobs. These jobs are disproportionately concentrated in the service sector, particularly in distribution, hotels and catering and in 'other services' both public and private. Temporary workers are primarily in lower skilled occupations but are also in some occupations which are more skilled, or, indeed, highly skilled. In these instances the skills concerned tend to be highly general - such as teaching or nursing skills - rather than skills specific to one employer.

The majority of temporary workers consider their jobs to be of a seasonal, temporary or casual nature rather than fixed-term contract jobs. However, those in the manufacturing sector and, more particularly, those in more highly skilled positions, are more likely to place themselves in the latter category. Temporary workers are rather more likely to be self-employed than is the generality of the labour force. A considerable proportion of self-employed temporary workers come from industries where the overall rate of self-employment is above average, such as construction, or have occupations best described as 'professional', although low skilled service and industrial workers are also to be found in large numbers amongst them. Agency workers and their close equivalents make up only a small minority of the temporary workforce and most of them are concentrated in a very narrow range of occupations, particularly those involving office or secretarial skills. The majority of temporary workers are simultaneously part-time workers and, especially for those in seasonal, temporary or casual jobs and employed in the service sector, the extent of overlap between temporary and part-time working is high. This provides support for the suggestion that in certain cases part-time and temporary workers are equivalents, and are viewed as such by employers and workers themselves.

Whilst many temporary workers are employed in small establishments, this seems to result from the industrial and occupational distribution of temporary working, rather than a greater propensity of small establishments to use such workers. Equally, there does not appear to be any great regional variation in the use of temporary workers, except that almost all agency workers are in the South East of the country.

Temporary workers are disproportionately women. This can be explained largely by the industrial and occupational distribution of the jobs which they have and by the overlap between part-time working and temporary working. Women temporary workers are more likely to have low skilled, part-time, seasonal, temporary or casual jobs, whilst men temporary workers are more likely to have more skilled, full-time, fixed-term contract jobs. Teenagers are also heavily over-represented amongst the temporary labour force; a substantial number of them are still at school and are working part-time. People over retirement age are somewhat over-represented in the temporary labour force, and many of them too are part-time workers.

The single most important reason given by temporary workers for working on that basis is that a permanent job could not be found. Nevertheless, it is the reason offered by only just over one third of all temporary workers. Men, those working full-time and those with fixed-term contracts, are more likely to have taken a temporary job because they had been unable to find a permanent job and thus can be thought of as 'involuntary' temporary workers. Women (particularly married women), those with part-time and those with seasonal, temporary or casual jobs, are more likely to have taken a temporary job because they did not want a permanent job and thus can be thought of as 'voluntary' temporary workers. Taking a temporary job because it was associated with a course of training was a reason offered by some young persons, although even among them the proportion is not large. One in eight of all temporary workers are participants in special government schemes offering jobs or workplace-based training to the otherwise unemployed. For young people, particularly teenagers, this form of temporary job is of very great importance. Indeed, that part of the over-representation of teenagers amongst the temporary labour force which is not explained by the temporary working of persons still at school is explained by the high proportion of the age group in special youth training schemes.

Finally, once account is taken of the major expansion of special employment programmes, particularly job creation schemes, in recent years, the LFS provides no evidence of any growth in temporary working. Between 1983 and 1986, the only years for which comparable data is available, the total number of temporary workers other than participants in special programmes grew by just over five per cent. Expressed as a proportion of the total labour force the temporary labour force remained just about constant in size. This contradicts the claims of certain earlier studies.

Notes

1. According to thte LFS code book, temporary jobs in the first category can include jobs the termination of which 'is fixed for, by example, reaching a *certain date* or *completing an assignment*, or by return of an employee who has been temporarily replaced' (our italics) - i.e. jobs that could fit equally well into the second category - whilst jobs in the second category are taken to include those with 'a work contract for a *specific task* or a *fixed period of time*' (our italics) - i.e jobs that could fit equally well into the first category.

2. For the purposes of this paragraph we have conducted our analysis using the OPCS's KOS occupational grouping system rather than

the Warwick Institute of Employment's WOC system. The former separately identifies 161 occupations, the latter 24.

3. The most substantial difference is for lower grade personnel service occupations, where 65 per cent of all temporaries are in small establishments as opposed to 53 per cent of all workers.

4. Most of these young people would have had evening/weekend jobs and these, we suspect, were heavily concentrated in the retailing and catering industries. According to employers in the retailing sector contacted in the course of our case studies, such evening/weekend jobs are categorised as part-time, but the persons doing them do not have any special 'temporary' status.

5. This was not done in an initial analysis of LFS data on temporary working (MSC, 1985), which suggested that there had been an increase in the proportion of the labour force having temporary jobs from 5.9 per cent to 6.4 per cent between 1983 and 1984.

6. The 1981 LFS distinguished persons with 'an occasional or casual job (including seasonal workers)' from those with a 'regular job', but this was a much more restrictive definition of temporary work than used subsequently. We should therefore question the validity of attempts (for example, Hakim, 1987) to compare 1981 with later data.

7. Both Meager and LRD based their claims on surveys asking employers/local union officials how many temporary workers they employed/were employed now and one or two years previously. Estimates of the latter are notoriously unreliable. One study (CBI, 1983) has shown that a significant proportion of firms actually experiencing fairly large changes in their total workforces report in response to such questions that their workforces have 'stayed the same'. When an issue as much discussed as temporary working is the main subject of the survey, the extent of bias is likely to be even greater.

8. Econometric evidence in support of this - at least with respect to the demand for labour supplied by 'temporary help' firms (the equivalent of agencies in Britain) - has been presented by Joray

(1981) for the USA. Comparisons andd projections of 'temporary help' industry employment and total employment made by the US Bureau of Labour Statistics (see Carey/Hazelbaker, 1986) provide further indications of the validity of this thesis.

Table 2.1   Industrial distribution of temporary employment

Percentages

Industry (1980 SIC)	Prop. of emp. which is temp.	Prop. of total temp. emp.
(0) agric., forestry & fishing	8.0	3.1
(1) energy & water supply	3.1	1.5
(2) minerals & chemicals	3.1	1.7
(3) metals, eng. & vehicles	2.7	4.6
(4) other manufacturing	4.2	6.5
(5) construction	7.8	9.2
(6) distribution, hotels & catering	7.9	24.7
retail distribution (6.4-5)	8.0	13.5
hotels & catering (6.6)	11.6	8.5
(7) transport & communications	2.7	2.6
(8) banking, insurance, finance and business services	5.0	6.6
business services (8.3)	7.5	4.8
(9) other services	9.1	38.2
public admin. (9.1)	6.0	5.6
education (9.3)	11.1	11.4
medical services (9.5)	5.0	4.3
other services provided to general public (9.6)	9.7	4.9
recreational and other cultural services (9.7)	15.4	5.2
personal services (9.8)	10.4	2.0
domestic services (9.9)	25.6	3.1
(0-9) total	6.5	100.0
manufacturing (2-4)	3.4	12.9
services(6-9)	7.5	72.1

Source: 1984 LFS

Table 2.2 Occupational distribution of temporary employment

Percentages

Occupation (WOC)	Prop. of emp. which is temp.	Prop. of total temp. emp.
managerial and admin. group	3.2	7.1
of which		
managers & administrators	0.9	0.4
skilled personal service occups.	3.3	4.8
higher level service occupations	7.6	17.6
of which		
education profs.	13.4	8.7
health profs.	6.8	4.7
higher level indust. occups.	4.8	3.7
of which		
engineers, scientists	4.9	2.2
technicians etc	4.6	1.5
lower level service & supervisory occups.	8.1	37.3
of which		
clerical occups.	6.1	8.1
secretarial occups.	6.8	3.8
other sales occups.	12.8	10.1
supervisors	1.4	0.9
other personal service occups.	11.1	14.4
craft and foreman group	4.5	10.7
of which		
foremen	2.0	1.3
eng. craftsmen	4.1	4.0
lower level indust. & other occups.	7.0	23.2
of which		
other operatives	6.8	15.6
all occupations	6.4	100.0

Source: 1984 LFS

Table 2.3   Form of temporary employment by industry

Percentages

Industry (1980 SIC)	Proportion of temp. workers who are on a fixed contract	seasonal, temp. casual
(0) agric., forestry & fishing	30	70
(1) energy & water supply	59	41
(2) minerals & chemicals	28	72
(3) metals, eng. & vehicles	52	48
(4) other manufacturing	20	80
(5) construction	61	39
(6) distribution, hotels & catering	13	87
retail distribution (6.4-5)	12	88
hotels & catering (6.6)	6	94
(7) transport & communications	31	69
(8) banking, insurance, finance and business services	34	66
business services (8.3)	31	69
(9) other services	44	56
public admin. (9.1)	57	43
education (9.3)	47	53
medical services (9.5)	54	46
other services provided to general public (9.6)	42	58
recreational and other cultural services (9.7)	43	57
personal services (9.8)	28	72
domestic services (9.9)	8	92
(0-9) total	35	65
manufacturing (2-4)	33	67
services(6-9)	32	68

Source: 1984 LFS

Table 2.4   Form of temporary working by occupation

Percentages

Occupation (WOC)	Proportion of temp. workers who are	
	on a fixed contract	seasonal, temp. casual
managerial and admin. group	29	71
of which		
managers & administrators	62	38
skilled personal service occups.	66	34
higher level service occupations	55	45
of which		
education profs.	52	48
health profs.	55	45
higher level indust. occups.	81	19
of which		
engineers, scientists	82	18
technicians etc	80	20
lower level service & supervisory occups.	16	84
of which		
clerical occups.	28	72
secretarial occups.	20	80
other sales occups.	13	87
supervisors	19	81
other personal service occups.	11	89
craft and foreman group	63	37
of which		
foremen	64	36
eng. craftsmen	66	34
lower level indust. & other occups.	31	69
of which		
other operatives	26	74
all occupations	35	65

Source: 1984 LFS

Table 2.5   Occupational distribution of agency workers

Percentages

Occupation (KOS)	Prop. of total emp.	Prop. of all agency workers	Prop. of emp. which is temp.	Agency workers as prop. of all temps.
economists, statisticians, systems analysts, computer programmers	0.6	6.0	8	29
nurse administrators, nurses	2.6	9.3	6	14
draftsmen	0.4	4.4	8	29
clerks	7.4	10.4	7	21
secretaries, shorthand typists, receptionists	3.6	23.8	7	21
office machine operators	0.6	5.2	8	21
telephonists, radio and telegraph operators	0.5	5.8	6	48
bus, coach, lorry drivers	2.7	5.4	3	13
total of above occupations	18.4	70.3		
all occupations	100.0	100.0	6	3

Source: 1984 LFS

Table 2.6   Self-employed temporary workers by selected industry

Percentages

Industry (1980 SIC)		Prop. of total l.f. self-emp.	Prop. of temp. l.f. self-emp.	Prop. of all self-emp. temps.
(2-4)	manufacturing	4	14	12
(5)	construction	30	35	22
(6)	distribution, hotels & catering	17	10	16
	retail distrib. (6.4-5)	18	9	9
	hotels & catering (6.6)	16	7	4
(8)	banking, insurance, finance business services	12	23	10
(9)	other services	6	13	33
	recreational and other cultural servs. (9.7)	16	24	9
	personal services (9.8)	35	44	6
	domestic services (9.9)	19	32	7
(0-9)	total	11	15	100

Source: 1984 LFS

Table 2.7   Part-time temporary workers by selected occupation

Percentages

Occupation (WOC)	Prop. of total l.f. part-time	Prop. of temp. l.f. part-time	Prop. of all part-time temps
managerial and admin. group	13	61	8
of which			
mans. and administrators	2	25	-
skilled personal serv. occs.	16	54	5
higher level sev. occups.	19	54	18
of which			
education profs.	19	66	10
health profs.	32	45	4
higher level indust. occups.	3	18	1
of which			
engineers, scientists	3	23	-
technicians etc	3	11	-
lower level service and supervisory			
occups.	45	71	49
of which			
clerical occups.	26	44	6
secretarial occups.	37	59	4
other sales occups.	60	81	15
other personal serv. occs.	76	85	22
craft and foreman group	2	16	3
of which			
other operatives	12	50	14
all occupations	21	54	100

Source: 1984 LFS

Table 2.8   Female temporary workers by selected occupation

Percentages

Occupation (WOC)	Prop. of total l.f. female	Prop.of temp. l.f. female	Prop.of all temp. female
managerial and admin. group	34	77	10
of which			
mans. and administrators	8	25	-
skilled personal serv. occs.	6	79	7
higher level serv. occups.	49	66	21
of which			
education profs.	57	79	13
health profs.	74	67	6
higher level indust. occups.	9	1	1
of which			
engineers, scientists	5	12	-
technicians etc	14	13	-
lower level service and supervisory occups.	79	85	55
of which			
clerical occups.	76	83	12
secretarial occups.	98	99	7
other sales occup.	76	70	13
other personal serv. occs.	85	83	22
craft and foreman group	3	5	1
of which			
eng. craftsmen	1	1	-
lower level indust. & other occs.	24	27	12
of which			
other operatives	23	32	9
all occupations	41	54	100

Source: 1984 LFS

Table 2.9   Age distribution of temporary employment

Percentages

Age groups	Prop. of total emp.	Prop. of temp. emp.	Prop. of emp. which is temp.
16-19	8.0	29.3	23.5
20-24	12.6	12.7	6.5
25-34	22.1	19.4	5.6
35-44	23.7	17.8	4.8
45-54	19.5	9.7	3.2
55-59	7.8	3.8	3.1
60-64	4.7	3.1	4.2
65+	1.6	4.2	16.3
all ages	100.0	100.0	6.4

Source: 1984 LFS

Table 2.10   Reasons for taking temporary employment by characteristics of persons and jobs

Percentages

Characteristics of person/temp. job	Job incs. training	Couldn't find perm.job	Didn't want perm.job	Other/no reason
all	5.2	35.6	27.1	32.1
men	6.7	43.9	15.8	33.7
women	4.0	28.6	36.7	30.7
married women	1.2	24.7	42.7	31.3
full-time	10.2	50.7	8.3	30.8
part-time	0.9	22.8	43.2	33.1
fixed contract	12.9	40.7	10.0	36.4
seasonal/temp/casual	1.0	32.8	36.4	29.7
agency workers	0.6	33.2	38.4	26.8
self-employed	0.7	16.8	34.4	48.0
dep. employee	6.0	38.9	25.9	29.2
in spec. emp. measure	10.3	73.9	2.1	13.7
at school	0.3	1.2	54.2	44.3
retired	-	5.3	56.0	38.7

Source: 1984 LFS

Table 2.11   Reasons for taking temporary employment by age

Percentages

Age groups	Job incs. training	Couldn't find perm.job	Didn't want perm.job	Other/ no reason
all	5.2	35.6	27.1	32.1
16 - 19	8.4	37.9	26.9	26.8
20 - 24	15.1	45.4	13.7	25.8
25 - 34	2.7	36.6	27.2	33.5
35 - 44	0.9	33.7	27.2	38.2
45 - 54	1.0	37.5	27.1	34.4
55 - 59	0.6	32.8	29.7	36.9
60 - 64	0.8	20.3	40.3	38.6
65+	-	3.0	57.5	39.5

Source: 1984 LFS

Table 2.12   Proportion of temporary workers at school, in special employment measures and retired by age

Percentages

Age groups	At school	In spec. emp. measure	Retired
all	8.5	13.1	6.0
16 - 19	29.5	32.2	n.a.
19 - 24	n.a.	14.4	n.a.
25 - 29	n.a.	5.2	n.a.
30 - 59	n.a.	3.4	n.a.
60 - 64	n.a.	1.6	58.7
65+	n.a.	n.a.	100.0

n.a. = not appropriate

Source: 1984 LFS

Table 2.13 Temporary employment 1983-1986

000s and Percentages

	1983	1984	1985	1986
temp. workers*	1,253	1,299	1,314	1,320
total employment*	22,589	23,072	23,343	23,433
temps as proportion of total employment*	5.5	5.6	5.6	5.6

* Excluding participants in special employment measures

Source: 1983-86 LFS

3 Employers' use of temporary labour: results of an establishment survey

The only representative survey of users of temporary labour at present available is the PSI/Department of Employment/ACAS workplace industrial relations survey (WIRS). This was carried out with a sample of some 2,000 establishments in 1980 and in 1984 (see, Daniel/Millward, 1983; Millward/Stevens, 1986). For the purposes of this study a special analysis of the new 1984 data was undertaken.

WIRS is, as its name suggests, primarily concerned with industrial relations institutions and practices. It does, however, collect a limited amount of information on personnel practices, and as part of this has asked questions about the use of temporary workers. These are concerned with two specific types of temporary worker, persons on fixed-term contracts of less than 12 months (the then qualifying period for protection against unfair dismissal) and agency-supplied workers. The survey asks whether these categories of worker are, or have been, employed, and if so how many, but with reference to the previous month for the first category and the previous 12 months for the second category. As a consequence it provides a snapshot view of the use of the first category and is likely to understate the importance of fixed-term contract working insofar as this is a form of seasonal working. Since it was carried out over a four-month summer period (May-August), the practices of these industries with summer peaks will have been better captured than the practices of those with peaks at other times of the year.

Temporary workers hired for a fixed-term in excess of one year were not identified by WIRS, although other than in the academic/research area numbers so employed are likely to be small. More significantly the survey collected no information about temporary workers hired on open-ended or indefinite contracts, in order to meet exceptional needs whose precise duration could not be specified in advance. Our case studies [see Chapter 7] have shown that these might make up a not unimportant share of the temporary labour force. Equally, WIRS collected no information about casual workers although, as our analysis of the LFS suggests, they are also an important form of temporary worker, particularly in certain parts of the service sector [see Chapter 6]. Finally, it excludes entirely from its sampling frame establishments with less than 25 employees. From the LFS [Chapter 2] we have seen that these employ 50 per cent of all temporary workers, 38 per cent of all fixed-term contract workers and 18 per cent of all agency workers, compared to 37 per cent of all workers.

The 1980 WIRS also contained questions on the use of fixed-term contract and agency workers. The question about the first category was the same as the 1984 survey, but that about the second differed in that it was concerned with the use of agency workers in the previous month rather than the previous 12 months. This meant that the scope for comparing establishment behaviour over time, which would provide some indication of whether there has been any increase in the use of temporary workers [see Chapter 7], was rather limited. However, we were able to make comparisons for the use of fixed-term contract workers and we also report briefly the results of this exercise.

For the purposes of our analysis establishments were classified as being 'users' or 'non-users' of each of the two categories of temporary worker. This is admittedly a rather crude distinction, but one which could be justified by the very uneven break - some 80 per cent of establishments were 'non-users' for each category - which it produced[1]. For experimental purposes we also separated out 'high user' establishments where the number of fixed-term contract or agency workers used was the equivalent of five per cent or more of the labour force but the results thereby obtained were not more instructive than those obtained by the initial classification and so are reported upon only in a limited fashion. Since large establishments are more likely to have at least one temporary worker than small establishments (i.e. to be 'users'), we broke down our results according to establishment size where we thought this to be relevant. Because of the limitations of the package currently available for us to analyse WIRS data, we were restricted to cross-tabulations and the use of elementary confidence tests to examine the significance of the differences these revealed.

The extent of temporary working

In 1984, some 20-22 per cent of establishments made some use of each of the two categorised temporary workers in the relevant reference period, whilst some 6-7 per cent could be described as 'high users'. Table 3.1 gives the industrial distribution of user establishments. With respect to fixed-term contract workers, it appears that manufacturing establishments are much less likely than average and service sector establishments are rather more likely than average to make use of them. With agency workers the situation is reversed: manufacturing establishments are rather more likely than average and service establishments rather less likely than average to use them. An important determinant of this result is the behaviour of public sector establishments. Table 3.2 shows that there is no difference between private manufacturing and private service establishments in their use of fixed-term contract workers and agency workers. Whilst the nationalised industries appear similar to private manufacturing industry, employers in public administration are more likely to be using workers hired on fixed-term contracts. This last result is strongly determined by the practices of establishments in the educational and, to a lesser extent, health sectors (see Table 3.1), and is in conformity with the findings of the LFS which showed a disproportionate share of teachers and, to a lesser extent, medical staff employed in this fashion. On the other hand, and with the exception of medical services where, as the LFS also shows, use is made of agency nurses and doctors, public sector establishments of any kind are very much less likely to make use of agency workers[2]. The most important users of agency workers are establishments in the banking, insurance, finance and business services sector, again a result supporting the findings of our LFS analysis, and these are particularly concentrated in the business services sub-sector where agencies themselves are located.

Comparing, for fixed-term contract workers, the results of the 1984 survey with those of the 1980 survey we found that there had been little change. As Table 3.3 shows, the overall proportion of establishments using such workers stood at around 20 per cent in both years and the proportion of 'high users' at seven per cent. This was true for most industries, the only notable exceptions being a significant increase in the use of fixed-term contract workers in the minerals and chemicals industry, in banking, insurance and businesses services and in education (an increase in the proportion of 'high users' only), and a significant decrease in their use in the construction industry.

We are not able to account for these industry level changes, but find the broad picture of 'no change' of more importance. Insofar as a growth in the use of temporary workers in recent years has been proposed by certain commentators [see Chapter 2], this growth appears to have occurred largely in the manufacturing sector. It is here, as our LFS analysis and our case studies indicate, that fixed-term contracts are quite an important form of engagement for temporary workers. At least for the period 1980 to 1984, WIRS fails to offer substantiating evidence that there has been any growth in the use of this form of temporary worker. Any growth which has occurred must either have come later or have involved other forms of temporary working, such as the imposition of a special 'temporary' status on certain workers recruited on open-ended contracts - something which our case studies indicate *might* have been the case. On the other hand, the LFS data which encompassed such temporary working and which allowed the situation in 1986 to be compared to that in 1983, also showed no real growth in the proportion of the workforce in temporary employment.

Characteristics of users

As the 1984 survey made clear, there are important differences between the public and private sectors in their use of temporary workers. In addition, we know that most if not all of the public sector is subject to administrative rather than market forces and has its own peculiar system of industrial relations. We therefore decided to concentrate our analysis of the characteristics of users of temporary workers on private sector establishments. We separated private manufacturing and private service establishments where they appeared to differ from one another.

Previous studies of employers' use of temporary workers, both in this country (Meager, 1985) and in the United States (Magnum/Mayall/Nelson, 1986), have indicated that its likelihood increases with the size of the organisation. The reason for this, according to the second of the two studies just cited, is that 'large firms... had more rationalised hiring systems and were better able to identify when temporary workers could be used efficiently'. The WIRS data supported this proposition when the simple 'on-off' distinction between 'users' and 'non-users' was used. However, when the 'high use' of temporary workers was examined, there were no significant differences between establishments grouped according to size. Table 3.4 shows this. This result underlines the importance of employing a measure which takes account of the number of workers in question in relation to the total number of employees in the organisation when testing propositions about the influence of size on personnel practices.

Performance characteristics

Because of data limitations we were not able to see whether establishments which experienced (substantial) fluctuations in demand for their output were more likely to be greater than average users of temporary workers. However, it could be argued, as has been done in the related literature on labour hoarding (see Greer/Rhoades, 1977), that establishments in a dominant market position might develop the organisational capacity to maintain more stable employment in the face of demand fluctuations, and WIRS does provide management's assessment of sensitivity of output to price changes by competitors - a good indicator of the degree of market dominance. No clear relationship was established when we tested this proposition, and the separate analysis of manufacturing and service establishments did not alter the outcome[3]. It has also been argued, in discussions both of temporary employment (for example, Atkinson, 1984) and of labour hoarding (for example, Greer/Rhoades, 1977; Bowers/Deaton/Turk, 1982), that enterprises with a high capital-labour ratio or high degree of technical inflexibility are more likely to maintain stable employment relationships. WIRS gives information on labour costs as a proportion of total costs which we used as a proxy for information on capital intensity, but our analysis gave no indication that the predicted relationship did obtain. Inclusion of data on casual workers might have altered the picture, at least for the service sector.

As well as looking for associations between the degree of volatility of operations and the use of temporary workers, we were able to consider a number of performance indicators for establishments. As Table 3.5 makes clear, establishments where output is currently falling appear to be less likely to make use of fixed-term contract workers, although there is only a small, non-significant difference in this respect between establishments with rising and with stable output. In contrast, there is no clear relationship between changes in level of output and the use of agency workers, and a separate analysis of the sub-sectors of manufacturing and services did not alter this result. In a similar fashion, and as Tables 3.6 and 3.7 show, establishments where the workforce is declining, both in the long-term and the short-term, are less likely to be users of fixed-term contract workers. Again, the likelihood of the use of agency workers appears unaffected by labour force change. These findings suggest that fixed-term contract workers and agency workers are not always direct substitutes for one another (in other words, that resort to one might be made for reasons very different than resort to the other). They also provide some support for the thesis proposed by earlier studies of temporary workers (particularly Meager, 1985), where it has been argued that there is a strong association between growing organisations and users of temporary labour[4].

It also seemed interesting to see if there was any relationship between the use of overtime working and the use of temporary workers. No really clear picture was distinguishable, except for private manufacturing establishments where, as Table 3.8 suggests, establishments making less use of overtime are also less likely to be making use of fixed-term contract workers. The absence of difference in behaviour between those with increasing and those with constant overtime levels is, however, not surprising. Temporary workers and overtime working could be substitutes or complements (albeit that overtime often permits a more immediate response and entails no recruitment/training costs), and our case studies explore this issue in more detail.

Industrial relations characteristics

We sought to test the proposition that, as a result of union hostility to temporary workers, the likelihood of their use would be inversely related to the strength of unions in the establishment. The high level of usage of temporary workers in public administration, where union density is high and formal systems of negotiation and consultation firmly established, already suggests that the relationship is by no means as straightforward as the initial proposition implies, and this applies also to private sector establishments. Indeed, as Table 3.9 suggests, manufacturing establishments where trade unions were recognised were slightly more likely to use fixed-term contract workers than those where they were not recognised, and the predicted relationship held only for agency workers in service establishments. Equally, the degree of unionisation of the workforce seemed to have little impact on the personnel practices of manufacturing establishments in their use either of fixed-term contract workers or agency workers. In the service sector the predicted relationship appeared to obtain, but again only with respect to agency workers (Table 3.10). Since union recognition and union density are both positively related to establishment size (see Daniel/Millward, 1983), we tested to see if the above results were sustained when size was controlled for. In general they were, although small numbers in the (unweighted) sample meant that the differences revealed were not always significant. However, one finding was reversed. In large private manufacturing establishments where unions were recognised the use of agency workers was significantly lower (see Table 3.11).

It seems from these results that unions have a greater (negative) impact upon the use of agency workers than upon the use of fixed-term contract workers. This might be explained by the fact that the former category are not the direct employees of the establishment and that their terms and conditions of employment are less subject to regulation by unions. As such they are seen by them as a greater 'threat' than other forms of temporary worker. It would, however, have been interesting to see what relationships might have been revealed had WIRS picked up information on casual workers, since casual working (albeit involving direct employment) is also a considerably less regulated form of temporary working and gives an employer considerable disposition over his labour inputs. Again, we would expect its level of use to be inversely related to the level of union organisation in an establishment.

Finally, we sought the existence of any relationships between labour force structure and the use of temporary workers. The literature on both temporary working and labour-hoarding suggests that the higher the skill level, or more precisely the *specific* skill level, of his labour force, the more likely an employer is to seek to maintain continuity of employment and so protect the training investments he has made. Using one minus the proportion of the workforce holding unskilled, semi-skilled or clerical jobs as a proxy for the level of skill of the workforce, Table 3.12 suggests that, at least with fixed-term contract workers, employers' behaviour is as expected - establishments with a highly skilled labour force are less likely to use temporary workers. In the service sector, however, the relationship is the opposite: establishments with a low proportion of the labour force which is skilled are less likely to use fixed-term contract workers. One explanation for this might be that, rather than using this method to bring in temporary labour, service establishments with a predominantly low skilled labour force rely on casual workers. With agency workers the only clear relationship is for the service sector, and again the suggestion is that in establishments where a large proportion of the labour force is unskilled this form of labour is less likely to be found. The explanation is probably the same as for the sector's use of fixed-term contract workers - that casual workers are the principal form of temporary worker engaged.

It has been suggested by proponents of the theory of the 'flexible firm' that organisations making use of one form of flexible labour are also likely to make use of other forms of it (see, for example, Atkinson, 1984). We tried to test this hypothesis with respect to the use of three other forms of 'flexible labour', namely part-time workers, home workers and freelance workers by employers of temporary workers. In fact, we found that agency workers and part-time workers might to some extent be substitutes for one another, in that the higher the proportion of the work force that was part-time, the lower the likelihood that the establishment was using such temporary workers. This is shown in Table 3.13. Use of home workers was unrelated to use of temporary workers (Table 3.14), and only in the private service sector was there a clear and significant positive relationship between use of freelancers and use of agency workers (Table 3.15). Finally, although users of fixed-term contract workers were slightly more likely to use agency workers (and vice versa), as Table 3.16 shows, the relationship was barely a significant one. The global notion of the 'flexible firm' is therefore scarcely supported.

Conclusions

Whilst by no means an ideal data base, WIRS does provide the most extensive and most representative survey information currently available on employers' use of temporary labour in Britain. It is freer from selectivity bias than the recent survey conducted by the IMS (Meager, 1985) and, by covering a large number of employers/establishments, permits more detailed analysis. Its limitations are the lack of information on temporary workers employed on open-ended contracts and casual workers, on occupations of temporary workers, on employers' reasons for using such labour and on associated wage and other costs. Furthermore, WIRS's focus on matters other than employment practices means that information on certain useful contextual variables, particularly with respect to labour force structure and labour costs, was not available to test all the hypotheses the literature suggests.

Following the precedent of other studies, but also the dictates of the survey itself (which showed that most employers who do engage fixed-term contract or agency workers engage only one or two of them), we conducted our analysis largely in terms of a comparison of 'users' and 'non-users'. We looked at the industrial distribution of 'users', at whether there had been any increase in their numbers since 1980 and at differences between user and non-user establishments in terms of their size, output, performance, industrial relations and labour force characteristics. We found that only about one in five of all establishments used either form of temporary worker and only a third of those used them in numbers equivalent to at least five per cent of their labour forces. Manufacturing establishments were more likely to be users of agency workers, service establishments of fixed-term contract workers, although this difference was solely a consequence of the practices of public sector service establishments. As far as the use of fixed-term contract workers was concerned, for which consistent data was available, we found no indication that this had increased between 1980 and 1984. This is in apparent contradiction to the claims of some previous studies, but in line with data from the LFS.

Our investigations of characteristics of user establishments were made only for the private sector, since we assumed non-market forces to be of too great importance in the public sector to permit most of the relevant propositions to be tested. In line with other studies, we found that larger establishments were more likely to use temporary workers but, and more important, we also found that they were not more likely to be 'high users' of temporary workers. Because we had no direct measures of volatility in output or demand, we were not able to explore whether establishments experiencing important fluctuations in output or demand were also more important users of temporary labour. There was, however, no support for the proposition that establishments with a dominant market position or insensitive to their competitors' pricing behaviour were less likely to use temporary workers. Nor, at least for the manufacturing sector where the argument would seem most relevant, was there any evidence that more capital intensive establishments were less likely to be making use of such workers. A number of indicators suggested that where activity levels were declining temporary workers were less likely to be used. Thus, establishments with declining output, falling overtime and declining employment levels were less likely to use temporary workers or, more precisely, were less likely to be using fixed-term contract workers. Indeed, use of agency workers seemed totally unaffected by performance measured according to the above mentioned indicators. This suggests that these two forms of temporary labour are not usually functional equivalents.

In terms of the industrial relations context, the relationships found were not always those expected. At least in manufacturing, fixed-term contract workers were more likely to be found in establishments where unions had a higher level of membership or had been granted

Table 3.1 Proportion of establishments using fixed-term contract or agency workers by industry

Percentages

Industry (SIC, 1980)	User of ftc	High user* of ftc	User of agency	High user* of agency
(1) energy and water	12	1	19	*
(2) minerals and chems.	20	10	21	4
(3) metals, eng., vehicles	13	3	24	10
(4) other manufacturing	6	*	20	4
(5) construction	5	1	20	5
(6) distrib., hotels and catering	10	3	14	7
(7) transport and communications	6	1	10	4
(8) banking, insurance, finance, business services	15	4	34	16
(8.3-5) business services	17	5	46	28
(9) other services	37	16	10	3
(9.3) education	61	28	5	*
(9.5) medical services	26	6	32	14
(1-9) total	20	7	17	6
(2-4) manufacturing	11	3	22	6
(6-9) services	24	9	15	6

* Number of fixed-term contract/agency workers used equals at least five per cent of the labour force

Source: 1984 WIRS

Table 3.2   Proportion of establishments using fixed-term contract or agency workers by industry and ownership

Percentages

Industry/ownership	User of ftc	high user* of ftc	User of agency	High user* of agency
private manufacturing	11	3	22	7
private services	12	3	22	10
nationalised industries	13	1	9	3
public administration	39	17	8	2
total	20	7	17	6

* Number of fixed-term contract/agency workers used equals at least five per cent of the labour force

Source: 1984 WIRS

Table 3.3   Proportion of establishments using fixed-term contract workers in 1980 and 1984

Percentages

Industry (SIC, 1980)		User of ftc 1980	User of ftc 1984	High user* of ftc 1980	High user* of ftc 1984	(n) 1980	(n) 1984
(1)	energy and water	10	12	3	1	(38)	(44)
(2)	minerals and chems.	6	20	2	10	(67)	(81)
(3)	metals, eng., vehicles	9	13	1	3	(208)	(152)
(4)	other manufacturing	10	6	3	*	(233)	(194)
(5)	construction	18	5	7	1	(117)	(84)
(6)	distrib., hotels and catering	10	10	6	3	(432)	(365)
(7)	transport and communications	7	6	4	1	(110)	(127)
(8)	banking, insurance, finance, business services	6	15	4	4	(155)	(235)
	(8.3-5) bus. services	4	17	1	5	(86)	(121)
(9)	other services	39	37	12	16	(614)	(703)
	(9.3) education	60	61	21	28	(254)	(291)
	(9.5) medic.services	18	26	7	6	(60)	(60)
(1-9)	total	19	20	7	7	(1,976)	(1,985)
	(2-4) manufacturing	9	11	2	3	(508)	(427)
	(6-9) services	23	24	9	9	(1,311)	(1,429)

* Number of fixed-term contract workers used equals at least five per cent of the labour force

Source: 1980 and 1984 WIRS

Table 3.4a   Proportion of private sector establishments using fixed-term contract workers by size

Percentages

| | Size (number of employees) | | |
	25-99	100-499	500+
all private sector	(461)	(415)	(306)
user	10	23	35
high user*	3	4	3
private manufacturing	(148)	(219)	(222)
user	5	23	32
high user*	2	3	3
private services	(284)	(173)	(78)
user	12	24	41
high user*	4	5	1

* Number of fixed-term contract workers used equals at least five per cent of the labour force

Table 3.4b   Proportion of private sector establishments using agency workers by size

Percentages

| | Size (number of employees) | | |
	25-99	100-499	500+
all private sector	(459)	(407)	(300)
user	22	31	51
high user*	10	7	7
private manufacturing	(148)	(218)	(219)
user	21	32	51
high user*	9	6	7
private services	(283)	(166)	(75)
user	22	28	51
high user*	11	10	9

* Number of agency workers used equals at least five per cent of the labour force

Source: 1984 WIRS

Table 3.5a Proportion of private sector establishments using fixed-term contract workers by change in value of output/sales in past 12 months

Percentages

| | Output/sales | | | |
	Rising	Stable	Falling	Total
all private sector	12	10	4	11
	(731)	(352)	(127)	(1,266)
private manufacturing	12	10	6	11
	(234)	(129)	(49)	(423)
private services	14	11	2	12
	(462)	(188)	(71)	(762)

Excludes dk/na

Table 3.5b Proportion of private sector establishments using agency workers by change in value of output/sales in past 12 months.

Percentages

| | Output/sales | | | |
	Rising	Stable	Falling	Total
all private sector	21	22	19	22
	(725)	(347)	(126)	(1,254)
private manufacturing	24	15	24	22
	(234)	(127)	(49)	(421)
private services	21	26	14	22
	(456)	(186)	(70)	(754)

Excludes dk/na

Source: 1984 WIRS

Table 3.6a   Proportion of private sector establishments using fixed-term contract workers by change in numbers employed compred to one year ago

Percentages

	Employment change			
	Positive (more than 1%)	Stable (+1% to -1%)	Negative (more than -1%)	Total
all private sector	14 (528)	12 (330)	6 (408)	11 (1,266)
private manufacturing	17 (187)	5 (82)	6 (154)	11 (423)
private services	13 (298)	16 (228)	7 (236)	12 (762)

Excludes dk/na and establishments not existing one year ago

Table 3.6b   Proportion of private sector establishments using agency workers by change in numbers employed compared to one year ago

Percentages

	Employment change			
	Positive (more than 1%)	Stable (+1% to -1%)	Negative (more than -1%)	Total
all private sector	22 (524)	22 (327)	22 (404)	22 (1,254)
private manufacturing	20 (187)	25 (82)	23 (152)	22 (421)
private services	22 (294)	22 (226)	21 (234)	22 (754)

Excludes dk/na establishments not existing one year ago

Source: 1984 WIRS

Table 3.7a Proportion of private sector establishments using fixed-term contract workers by change in numbers employed compared to four years ago

Percentages

| | Employment change | | | |
	Positive (more than 5%)	Stable (+5% to -5%)	Negative (more than -5%)	Total
all private sector	15	12	6	11
	(408)	(397)	(461)	(1,266)
private manufacturing	15	12	7	11
	(129)	(92)	(203)	(423)
private services	16	13	6	12
	(251)	(286)	(226)	(762)

Excludes dk/na and establishments not existing four years ago

Table 3.7b Proportion of private sector establishments using agency workers by change in numbers employed compared to four years ago

Percentages

| | Employment change | | | |
	Positive (more than 5%)	Stable (+5% to -5%)	Negative (more than -5%)	Total
all private sector	24	22	20	22
	(404)	(392)	(457)	(1,254)
private manufacturing	22	19	23	22
	(129)	(92)	(200)	(421)
private services	26	22	17	22
	(247)	(282)	(224)	(754)

Excludes dk/na and establishments not existing four years ago

Source: 1984 WIRS

Table 3.8a Proportion of private sector establishments using fixed-term contract workers by changes in the level of overtime working compared to one year ago

Percentages

	Change in level of overtime			
	More	Same	Less	Total
all private sector	12	12	7	11
	(270)	(720)	(187)	(1,266)
private manufacturing	12	12	7	11
	(147)	(169)	(94)	(423)
private services	12	13	7	12
	(106)	(499)	(90)	(762)

Excludes dk/na and establishments without paid overtime

Table 3.8b Proportion of private sector establishments using agency workers by changes in the level of overtime working compared to one year ago

Percentages

	Change in level of overtime			
	More	Same	Less	Total
all private sector	26	19	21	22
	(268)	(711)	(187)	(1,254)
private manufacturing	25	18	23	22
	(147)	(168)	(94)	(421)
private services	18	18	19	22
	(106)	(491)	(90)	(754)

Excludes dk/na and establishments without paid overtime

Source: 1984 WIRS

Table 3.9a   Proportion of private sector establishments using fixed-term contract workers by whether trade unions recognised or not

Percentages

| | Union recognition | | |
	Some recognition	No recognition	Total
all private sector	11	11	11
	(603)	(663)	(1,266)
private manufacturing	13	8	11
	(235)	(188)	(423)
private services	12	13	12
	(328)	(434)	(762)

Excludes dk/na

Table 3.9b   Proportion of private sector establishments using agency workers by whether trade unions recognised or not

Percentages

| | Union recognition | | |
	Some recognition	No recognition	Total
all private sector	21	23	22
	(602)	(652)	(1,254)
private manufacturing	25	18	22
	(235)	(186)	(421)
private services	15	27	22
	(327)	(427)	(754)

Excludes dk/na

Source: 1984 WIRS

Table 3.10a Proportion of private sector establishments using fixed-term contract

Percentages

| | Level of union membership | | | |
	None (no membs.)	Low (less than 50%)	High (50% or more)	Total
all private sector	11 (533)	11 (262)	11 (346)	11 (1,266)
private manufacturing	9 (141)	9 (97)	11 (158)	11 (423)
private services	12 (366)	13 (133)	10 (178)	12 (762)

Excludes dk/na

Table 3.10b Proportion of private sector establishments using agency workers by level of union membership

Percentages

| | Level of union membership | | | |
	None (no membs.)	Low (less than 50%)	High (50% or more)	Total
all private sector	23 (527)	25 (260)	15 (347)	22 (1,254)
private manufacturing	16 (140)	38 (96)	15 (158)	22 (421)
private services	27 (362)	17 (132)	13 (178)	22 (954)

Excludes dk/na

Source: 1984 WIRS

Table 3.11a Proportion of private sector establishments using fixed-term contract workers by whether trade unions recognised or not and size

Percentages

| | Union recognition | | | |
	Some recognition		No recognition	
private manufacturing				
25-99 employees	4	(75)	7	(73)
100-499 employees	26	(177)	12	(42)
500+ employees	33	(214)	25	(8)
private services				
25-99 employees	12	(123)	12	(161)
100-499 employees	27	(91)	21	(82)
500+ employees	39	(51)	44	(27)

Excludes dk/na

Table 3.11b Proportion of private sector establishments using agency workers by whether trade unions recognised or not and size

Percentages

| | Union recognition | | | |
	Some recognition		No recognition	
private manufacturing				
25-99 employees	25	(75)	16	(73)
100-499 employees	30	(178)	43	(40)
500+ employees	49	(211)	100	(8)
private services				
25-99 employees	15	(124)	28	(159)
100-499 employees	26	(88)	31	(78)
500+ employees	50	(50)	52	(25)

Excludes dk/na

Source: 1984 WIRS

Table 3.12a Proportion of private sector establishments using fixed-term contract workers by skill level of labour force

Percentages

| | Proportion of labour force skilled* | | | |
	Low (less than 30%)	medium (30% to 70%)	High (more than 70%)	Total
all private sector	8	14	11	11
	(422)	(517)	(327)	(1,266)
private manufacturing	15	12	3	11
	(120)	(198)	(105)	(423)
private services	5	17	16	12
	(294)	(279)	(190)	(762)

Excludes dk/na

* 1 minus proportion of labour force unskilled, semi-skilled and clerical

Table 3.12b Proportion of private sector establishments using agency workers by skill level of labour force

Percentages

| | Proportion of labour force skilled* | | | |
	Low (less than 30%)	medium (30% to 70%)	High (more than 70%)	Total
all private sector	16	26	23	22
	(421)	(508)	(325)	(1,254)
private manufacturing	15	28	19	22
	(120)	(196)	(105)	(421)
private services	17	26	24	22
	(293)	(272)	(189)	(754)

Excludes dk/na

* 1 minus proportion of labour force unskilled, semi-skilled and clerical

Source: 1984 WIRS

Table 3.13a Proportion of private sector establishments using fixed-term contract workers by share of labour force working part-time

Percentages

| | Proportion working part-time | | | |
	Low (5% or less)	Medium 6% to 40%)	High (more than 40%)	Total
all private sector	11	11	11	11
	(577)	(468)	(177)	(1,266)
private manufacturing	12	8	*	11
	(257)	(146)	(7)	(423)
private services	11	13	11	12
	(256)	(315)	(171)	(762)

Excludes dk/na

Table 3.13b Proportion of private sector establishments using agency workers by share of labour force working part-time

Percentages

| | Proportion working part-time | | | |
	Low (5% or less)	Medium 6% to 40%)	High (more than 40%)	Total
all private sector	28	18	14	22
	(569)	(466)	(177)	(1,254)
private manufacturing	24	18	2	22
	(256)	(145)	(7)	(421)
private services	31	18	14	22
	(250)	(315)	(170)	(754)

Excludes dk/na

Source: 1984 WIRS

Table 3.14a Proportion of private sector establishments using fixed-term contract workers by use of home workers

Percentages

	With home workers	Without home workers	Total
all private sector	10	11	11
	(74)	(1,192)	(1,266)
private manufacturing	6	11	11
	(51)	(371)	(422)
private services	19	12	12
	(23)	(740)	(763)

Excludes dk/na

Source: 1984 WIRS

Table 3.14b Proportion of private sector establishments using agency workers by use of home workers

Percentages

	With home workers	Without home workers	Total
all private sector	23	22	22
	(74)	(1,180)	(1,254)
private manufacturing	17	23	22
	(51)	(370)	(421)
private services	37	21	22
	(23)	(731)	(792)

Excludes dk/na

Source: 1984 WIRS

Table 3.15a Proportion of private sector establishments using fixed-term contract workers by use of freelancers

Percentages

	With free-lancers	Without free-lancers	Total
all private sector	13	11	11
	(239)	(1,019)	(1,258)
private manufacturing	7	12	11
	(84)	(335)	(419)
private services	17	11	12
	(138)	(624)	(762)

Excludes dk/na

Table 3.15b Proportion of private sector establishments using agency workers by use of freelancers

Percentages

	With free-lancers	Without free-lancers	Total
all private sector	28	21	22
	(232)	(1,015)	(1,247)
private manufacturing	27	20	21
	(84)	(335)	(419)
private services	30	20	22
	(134)	(620)	(754)

Excludes dk/na

Source: 1984 WIRS

Table 3.16a Proportion of private sector establishments using fixed-term contract workers by use of agency workers

Percentages

	With agency workers	Without agency workers	Total
all private sector	14	10	11
	(277)	(977)	(1,254)
private manufacturing	14	10	11
	(92)	(328)	(421)
private services	15	11	12
	(164)	(590)	(754)

Excludes dk/na

Table 3.16b Proportion of private sector establishments using agency workers by use of fixed-term contract workers

Percentages

	With ftc workers	Without ftc workers	Total
all private sector	28	21	22
	(139)	(1,115)	(1,254)
private manufacturing	28	21	22
	(45)	(376)	(421)
private services	28	21	22
	(91)	(663)	(754)

Excludes dk/na

Source: 1984 WIRS

4 The unemployed and temporary jobs

This chapter addresses two questions: first, how important temporary jobs are as a step into employment for unemployed people; second, to what extent the ending of temporary jobs is an important reason for becoming unemployed? A third, technical question - how temporary jobs affect rights to unemployment compensation and under what circumstances they open new rights to benefits - is dealt with in an appendix.

Much of this chapter will draw upon an analysis of two large scale data sets - the Labour Force Survey, described in Chapter 1, and PSI's own Unemployed Flow Survey. This latter is a longitudinal survey over a period of two and a half years following a structured sample of some 4,000 persons who registered as unemployed in May 1980. We also draw upon the findings of an earlier longitudinal study of men registering as unemployed in 1978 - the Department of Health and Social Security's (DHSS) Cohort Study - which contributes information pertinent to the second of the two issues under consideration.

Temporary work as a way out of unemployment
It has frequently been argued that temporary jobs, although possibly less desirable than permanent jobs, do provide a form of work for otherwise unemployed people and, furthermore, one that enhances their chances of subsequently obtaining permanent jobs (Syrett, 1985). Not

only is having had some form of employment considered to increase a job seeker's attractiveness to an employer and diminish the chances of a devaluation of his work skills, but temporary placings themselves can turn into permanent ones, either because the temporary position is made permanent or because the employer becomes acquainted with the capabilities of the temporary worker and recruits him into a vacant permanent position.[1] Special temporary employment schemes such as the Community Programme are often justified in this manner, the suggestion being that they raise the chances of the long-term unemployed finding jobs some threefold (Turner, 1985). Equally, the temporary employment businesses make reference to a share of their workers subsequently being offered permanent jobs by the organisations with which they have been placed (FPS, 1983).

The importance of temporary jobs as a way back into work for persons who have been unemployed can be seen by reference to both the LFS and PSI's Unemployed Flow Survey. The LFS shows that a quarter of all persons who had been unemployed 12 months before the survey, but who were in work on the survey date, had temporary jobs, compared with just over three per cent who had been in work on both dates. The Unemployed Flow Survey also shows that, of those people who found work within 10 months of their initial registration as unemployed, a quarter took jobs which were temporary, temporary here meaning jobs with a predetermined end or date of termination. As many as 35 per cent took jobs which they regarded as 'stop-gap' or in which they intended to stay for only a short period.

Both surveys also suggest that the state of the local labour market has an important influence on the extent to which unemployed people take temporary work. We can see this indirectly from the LFS data which shows that the proportion of temporary working which is 'involuntary' (the proportion of temporary workers taking a temporary job because they were unable to find a permanent job) is highest in those regions where unemployment too is highest. Table 4.1 illustrates this.

We can see from the Unemployed Flow Survey that the proportion of people finding work within 10 months of registration as job seekers who took temporary jobs varied with the level of unemployment in their area. Only 18 per cent of those living in areas of 'low' unemployment took first jobs which were temporary, but 26 per cent of those living in areas of 'medium' unemployment and 33 per cent in areas of 'high' unemployment did so. Table 4.2, which illustrates this, also shows that the state of the local labour market made little difference to the proportion regarding their first jobs as 'stop-gap'. This suggests that in more favourable employment conditions it is easier to find a permanent job from which to continue one's job search - in other words, that the search could take place from a more secure base.

Temporary work as a way into unemployment

Temporary work seems to have an important role to play in the transition from unemployment to employment. However, it is also interesting to examine its role in the transition from employment to unemployment, both to see if those finishing temporary assignments are over-represented amongst people becoming jobless, and more particularly to see if temporary working is related to the phenomenon of recurrent unemployment. It has been suggested that the experience of repeated, if relatively short, spells of unemployment is as great a problem as the experience of single, long spells, and that precisely because temporary work is the way in which many of the unemployed re-enter work, it might increase the chance of unemployment being repeated (OECD, 1985).

The LFS provides some information on how far the ending of temporary jobs contributed to unemployment in Spring 1984. It shows that for those people without work and looking for a job, the ending of a temporary job was the second most important reason for having left their last employment. It was given by about 16 per cent of all concerned. However, it was less important than the main reasons - redundancy or dismissal - which together were given by 42 per cent. The ending of a temporary job was of greatest importance for unemployed teenagers. Just over a quarter of them (26 per cent) had left their last jobs for this reason, and only just over one third (35 per cent) because of redundancy or dismissal. Its importance sharply decreased for those in their early 20s, to stand at little above the average and fell gradually as age increased, to reach just over eight per cent for over-55 year olds.

The evidence from longitudinal surveys of the unemployed appears at first sight to be not wholly consistent. The Unemployed Flow Survey (see Daniel, 1981) suggests the contribution of the ending of temporary jobs to flows into unemployment is small. Of the three quarters (78 per cent) of those registering as unemployed who had previously been in work, only six per cent volunteered that they had become unemployed as the result of a temporary job coming to an end. Redundancies, which accounted for 37 per cent of job losses, dismissals, which accounted for nearly 15 per cent, and voluntary resignations, which accounted for another 37 per cent, were all more important. Only in areas of very high unemployment was there any substantial proportion for whom the ending of temporary jobs was the reason for unemployment (it was given by nearly 14 per cent of the sample in areas where unemployment was at least twice as high as the national average). It was also given more often (in 11 per cent of cases) by lower grade white collar workers, but this probably reflects the occupational distribution of temporary jobs.

A rather different picture is given by another longitudinal survey of the unemployed, the DHSS's Cohort Study. Amongst those men who had had a job immediately before registration, the coming to an end of a temporary job was the most important reason for their becoming unemployed. Some 21 per cent of all flows into unemployment by men who had previously been employed were accounted for in this way, slightly more than were accounted for by redundancy (20 per cent) or dissatisfaction with pay or conditions (19 per cent) and considerably more than were accounted for by dismissals (10 per cent) (Wood, 1982). Of the temporary jobs concerned, nearly three quarters (70 per cent) had been for six months or less (Stern, 1982). Since the Unemployed Flow Survey reported no significant difference between men and women in this respect, the variation in the results obtained from the Cohort Study cannot be accounted for by its concentration on men. However, it seems that the Cohort Study probed deeper into reasons for job loss, and that some of those whose unemployment was the consequence of a temporary job coming to an end might, without such probing, have classified themselves as 'redundant'. The total of redundancies and temporary jobs coming to an end was very similar in both surveys (43 per cent in the Unemployed Flow Survey and 41 per cent in the Cohort Study).

Insofar as they shed light on the problem of recurrent unemployment, the findings of longitudinal studies again appear inconsistent. The DHSS's Cohort Study suggests that those people who suffered recurrent unemployment in the year after registration were no more likely to have become unemployed initially because of a temporary job coming to an end. Furthermore, it suggest that those people who had become unemployed because of a temporary job coming to an end were just as likely to be unemployed for only a short spell and then to go back to work, and that they were less likely to have been continuously unemployed throughout the following year (Moylan/Millar/Davies, 1984).

Our special analysis of the Unemployed Flow Survey revealed a rather different state of affairs. The proportion of people initially becoming unemployed as a result of the coming to an end of a temporary job who found a new job within 10 months of initial registration was not markedly different from the proportion applying to the total sample, even after taking age into account. In other words, it did not appear that the ending of a temporary job increased the likelihood of long-term unemployment. The ending of a temporary job did, however, seem to contribute to recurrent unemployment. Those who became unemployed as a result of the ending of a temporary job, but who did not become long-term unemployed, were more likely to have experienced three or more spells of joblessness and to have had three or more jobs in the 20 months following initial registration than were the sample as a whole. This is shown in Table 4.3. Controlling for the intervening variables of age and sex did not seem to affect these findings. When we examined the larger sample of people whose first jobs after initial unemployment we obtained a very similar picture of a positive relationship between temporary working and recurrent unemployment. Table 4.4 shows this. When age, sex, skill level and state of the local labour market were taken into account, the findings were not affected. Equally, and as can be seen from Table 4.5, those who took first jobs that were temporary spent more of the 20 month observation period being unemployed and less of it in full-time employment than did those who took first jobs that were permanent.

Finally, a remarkably clear finding of the Unemployed Flow Survey is the way in which those who initially became unemployed as a result of the ending of a temporary job were much more likely than any other category in the sample to re-enter employment via a temporary job. As Table 4.6 shows, nearly 44 per cent of them did so, whilst the average for the sample was only 25 per cent. Moreover, although their new jobs were temporary, not all of them regarded them as a 'stop-gap'. Unlike the sample as a whole, for whom the proportion with 'stop-gap' first jobs was higher than the proportion with temporary first jobs, for those initially becoming unemployed as a result of the ending of a temporary job it was lower (38 per cent). This could suggest that, for such people, temporary working was more generally accepted as the norm.

Conclusions

This chapter has looked at the importance of temporary jobs as a source of flows both from unemployment into employment and from employment into unemployment. With respect to the first, we cited commentators who have argued that temporary jobs, by providing experience of recent working, increase an unemployed person's competitivenesson the labour market. We also drew on survey evidence to show that temporary work provided an important source of new jobs for unemployed people, of whom perhaps a quarter took such work. The higher the level of unemployment in the local labour market, the higher the proportion.

With respect to the coming to an end of a temporary job as a source of flows into unemployment, available evidence provided a rather unclear picture. Redundancy and dismissal were, not surprisingly, the most important reasons for job loss, but one survey found as much as one in five people who entered into unemployment did so after finishing a temporary job, whilst another put the proportion at only six per cent. It seems likely that the first of these surveys probed reasons for job loss more deeply than the latter, and that the second's estimates are too low.

We also tried to see if there was any relationship between temporary working and recurrent unemployment. Again, survey evidence was not always consistent. However, an important data set did give clear indications that, although not increasing the likelihood of long-term unemployment, temporary working was linked to recurrent unemployment. Both people entering unemployment as a result of losing a temporary job and people taking temporary jobs as a way out of unemployment seemed more likely to have taken a number of jobs, to have experienced a number of spells of unemployment, to have had less time in work and more time in unemployment than people becoming unemployed for other reasons, or managing to obtain a permanent job on leaving unemployment. Moreover, people entering unemployment because a temporary job had come to an end were more likely to leave unemployment via another temporary job.

These last findings should not, however, be taken to suggest that temporary working is a *cause* of recurrent unemployment or of unstable employment patterns. The survey upon which these findings were based did not provide sufficient details of personal characteristics for us to be able to take account of the influences certain of these might have exerted. Nor did it provide the detailed information on local labour markets, particularly at the occupational level, that would have been necessary to make a fuller judgement. Our case studies [see Chapters 5-7], which make reference to the environment in which users of temporary labour are operating, give some indication of the importance of alternative employment opportunities (or the lack of them) in explaining the labour market behaviour of at least some temporary workers.

Appendix: temporary working and rights to unemployment compensation

Unemployed people in Britain are eligible for one or both of two forms of benefit. Those who throughout the previous tax year have paid social security contributions as dependent employees (or, as a consequence of being registered as unemployed, have had these credited for them) are entitled to draw flat rate Unemployment Benefit for a period of one year. Those who have no or only an inadequate contributions record, and those who have exhausted their rights to Unemployment Benefit, can make a claim for means-tested Supplementary Benefit. Unemployed people with a working spouse are unable to draw this benefit, since the means test is applied to joint income. Unemployment Benefit recipients with a spouse who is not working will usually have an income low enough for those who qualify for topping-up Supplementary Benefit. In fact, it is only certain single unemployed people who are wholly reliant upon Unemployment Benefit; most of the registered unemployed are dependent, wholly or in part, on Supplementary Benefit (see *Social Security Statistics*, 1986).

Almost any job which a benefit recipient takes will have some effect upon his current entitlement to unemployment compensation. Unemployment Benefit is calculated on a daily basis, so that each day on which an Unemployment Benefit recipient works is a day for which he is not entitled to claim any benefit. Nevertheless, a very short-term job - lasting less than a week - can be to his financial advantage. This is not the case for persons in receipt of Supplementary Benefit. Supplementary Benefit is calculated on a weekly basis and is reduced by the equivalent of any earnings in the week that are in excess of £4. Most of the registered unemployed are unlikely to be interested in temporary jobs lasting only a few days. If they do take them they have little to gain by declaring the fact. Such jobs are more likely to be attractive to the unregistered, or uncompensated unemployed, or to people normally outside the labour force.

Temporary jobs lasting more than a week can be considered in terms of whether they open or reopen rights to Unemployment Benefit. Whether they do or not depends on their duration and the personal circumstances of the individual. Those currently in receipt of Unemployment Benefit, in other words those who have been unemployed for less than one year, can reopen rights to a further year of unemployment benefit if they work in insured employment for at least eight weeks. (According to the so-called 'linking rule', a spell of employment lasting less than this time is considered an *interruption* to a single spell of unemployment, whilst a spell of employment lasting longer than this but then coming to an end opens up a *new* spell of unemployment.) However, those who have exhausted their rights to Unemployment Benefit, in other words who have been unemployed for longer than one year, have to work for at least 13 weeks. Those with no record of social security contributions, in other words new entrants to the labour market, have to work at least 26 weeks if they are to be eligible for Unemployment Benefit when they lose their jobs. The regulations determining how short spells of employment affect subsequent rights to Unemployment Benefit are often unclearly presented, even in specialist publications (for example, Smith/Rowland, 1986). In some cases, important labour market actors are uncertain of them, and in the course of certain of our case studies [see Chapter 7] we found them to be a source of confusion.

Temporary workers who are also seasonal workers face special restrictions on their rights to Unemployment Benefit. According to social security legislation, a 'seasonal worker' is a 'person whose employment is for part or parts only of the year and those parts fall at approximately the same time each year.' By case law the definition applies when this pattern has existed for three years or more. However, a person is not treated as a seasonal worker if his off-season, or off-seasons in aggregate, do not exceed seven weeks. To draw unemployment benefit in an off-season a seasonal worker must show he has already had, or can reasonably expect to obtain, a substantial amount of employment during the current off-season - normally at least one quarter of that period. If, in a time of reduced employment opportunities, unemployed people rather than more traditional seasonal workers are filling a share of seasonal jobs, and if they develop a pattern of working in this fashion, they could be penalised by these regulations (see Hansard, 4/2/87).

Notes:

1. Our case studies provided further confirmation of this. Most employers spoken to made clear that, were permanent vacancies to arise, temporary workers would be in the best position to compete for them since they were known to the organisation.

Table 4.1 'Involuntary' temporary workers by region

	Unemploy-ment rate (%)	Ranking	Prop. of temps who are 'involuntary'(%)	Ranking
Northern	16	1	51	2
Scotland	15	2	47	1
Wales	14	3	47	3
North West	14	3	46	4
West Midlands	14	3	44	5
Yorks and Humberside	12	6	42	6
East Midlands	10	7	32	8
East Anglia	8	8	32	7
South West	8	8	30	9
South East	8	8	23	10

Source: 1984 LFS   rs=0.68, sig. at 0.01

Table 4.2 Permanence of first job by level of unemployment in local labour market

Percentages

Level of unemployment		First Job			
		Tempo-rary	Not temporary	Stop-gap	Expect to stay
low	(508)	17.9	81.6	37.7	61.6
medium	(661)	26.1	73.1	34.2	64.8
high	(515)	32.7	65.2	34.2	61.7
all	(1,695)	25.3	73.7	35.2	63.1

Source: PSI Unemployed Flow Survey

Table 4.3   Indicators of recurrent unemployment by reason for unemployment

Percentages

	All finding job in 10 months	of which reason for leaving last job/previous status				
		Redun-dant	End of contract	Dis-missed	Own accord	Not in work
proportion with 3 or more spells of unemployment	10.3	11.8	21.1	17.0	8.4	3.6
proportion with 3 or more jobs	13.2	15.8	28.2	12.5	11.7	6.5
	(1,023)	(364)	(57)	(109)	(296)	(166)

Source: PSI Unemployed Flow Survey

Table 4.4   Indicators of recurrent unemployment by nature of first job

Percentages

	All finding job in 10 months	of which first job	
		Temporary	Permanent
proportion with 3 or more spells of unemployment	10.3	18.2	7.5
proportion with 3 or more jobs	13.2	19.2	10.1
	(1,023)	(243)	(772)

Source: PSI Unemployed Flow Survey

Table 4.5   Duration of selected activities by nature of first job

Percentages

	All finding job in 10 months	of which first job	
		Temporary	Permanent
months in full-time work	12.05	10.24	12.61
standard error	(0.22)	(0.43)	(0.25)
months in unemployment	6.08	7.40	5.63
standard error	(0.18)	(0.38)	(0.21)

Source: PSI Unemployed Flow Survey

Table 4.6   Nature of first job by reason for unemployment

Percentages

	All finding job in 10 months	of which reason for leaving last job/previous status				
		Redun-dant	End of contract	Dis-missed	Own accord	Not in work
temporary	25.3	28.6	44.6	25.3	19.2	25.8
permanent	73.7	69.1	55.4	74.3	80.8	74.2
stop-gap	35.2	36.3	37.6	36.5	33.3	36.6
expect to stay	63.1	61.0	59.4	63.5	65.9	60.9
	(1,695)	(562)	(92)	(186)	(499)	(305)

Source: PSI Unemployed Flow Survey

5 Agency working

As our analysis of the Labour Force Survey in Chapter 2 showed, most temporary working involves people who are engaged and remunerated directly by the organisation where they work, either as dependent employees or on a casual or freelance/self-employed basis. A small proportion involves those who are engaged indirectly, their services being obtained from other organisations which are responsible for their remuneration and which charge the client organisation a fee. This form of temporary working we shall call 'agency working'. As we saw in Chapter 1, it is possible to distinguish two categories of temporary worker supplied via an intermediary - 'agency workers' and 'employees of works contractors'. Labour law accords very different rights to each category.

We start this chapter by looking more closely at the legal distinction between these two categories of temporary worker and go on to examine whether, in many cases of agency working, it is a meaningful one in practice. This leads to a discussion of the characteristics of the agency labour force and of the nature of the occupation and regional labour markets in which they are found. We look briefly at the phenomenon of 'temping' by secretarial/office staff in the South East of England, before concentrating in some detail on the particular case of contract computer staff. On the basis of our investigations we attempt to assess the extent of employment security enjoyed by these two groups of temporary workers.

Agency working in law and in practice

An 'agency' (or 'employment business' in the words of the 1973 Employment Agencies Act) is a 'business ... supplying persons in the employment of the person carrying on the business, to act for, and under the control of, other persons in any capacity' (S.13 (3)),[1] but the word 'employment' is used in a much wider sense than that of having a contract of employment. Although most agency workers are taxed and pay social security contributions as if they were dependent employees, and most think of themselves as an employee of the agency for which they work, the relationship between them and these agencies has been deemed not to be one of employment. Courts have reached this conclusion by arguing first, that there is no mutuality of obligation between agency and worker to provide and accept work and second, that the agency does not 'control' the work of the agency worker - this control is exercised by the client organisation to which the agency worker has been supplied (see Leighton, 1985a). A 'works contractor', on the other hand, is an organisation which supplies its own employees to undertake work at the premises of a client and which retains control over them whilst they are working there. A 'temporary services business', which specifies that persons working for it are under its 'direction, supervision and control', is not an 'employment business' in the terms of the Employment Agencies Act and is not subject to the regulations governing the operation of such businesses which the Act lays down.

The reasoning of the courts in denying employee status to agency workers has been criticised by some academic lawyers as a failure to accept the reality of their objective situation.[2] Equally important is the fact that in some cases the operations of 'agencies' and 'works contractors' are virtually identical. We can see this by reference to the Manpower Group. Manpower, along with Brook Street, Alfred Marks and Reed, is one of the four major suppliers of temporary staff in Britain (Key Note, 1985). Like other such suppliers of temporary staff, it pays its temporaries on the basis of hours worked. Equally, most of its assignments involve only one person, rather than a group or team, and most are rather short - about three-quarters are of two weeks duration or less (interviews with Manpower and the Federation of Recruitment and Employment Services (FRES)). However, it is not an 'agency', it is a 'works contractor', and its 'temporaries' all have indefinite contracts of employment (see Isaac, 1985).[3] These contracts, whilst stating it is a condition of employment that staff accept 'all reasonable assignments', make clear that the organisation has no obligation to offer work and that staff will not be paid when there is no work for them (the organisation refers to this as 'laying the worker off'). In addition, although they make clear that the workers are subject to Manpower's 'direction, supervision and control', they contain a clause of delegation. Employees are informed that 'where the job involves working with people employed by the ... client, then naturally you should be prepared to carry out instructions from anyone authorised by the client, where this is necessary to do the work'.

More confusing still are the practices of the agencies themselves. Many refer to their agency workers, at least informally, as their 'employees'. In the past it seems a lot went further and either provided the workers with documentation of their relationship which labelled them as employees or, and contrary to the requirements of the Employment Agencies Act, failed to specify that they were not. There are indications that this at last is changing, partly because of the court cases of the last few years. These have led the body representing the interests of the agencies (and private placement bureaux), the Federation of Recruitment and Employment Services (FRES), to advise its members to make explicit in all documentation given to their temporary staff that they have no obligation to provide them with work and, more important, that the relationship they have with them is not one of employment (interview with FRES).[4]

At the same time, however, there have been developments which appear to run in the opposite direction and which reinforce the appearance of employee status. The larger agencies supplying secretarial and office staff in the metropolitan areas, primarily because they are competing with one another for scarce labour, are increasingly offering the sort of fringe benefits associated with employment. These include sick pay, holiday pay, service related increments and even training courses (particularly for word processing staff). Manpower told us that its staff are attracted to it and stay with it because of the level of such fringe benefits and the level of pay it offers and not because they are given contracts which confirm them as having dependent employee status.

The phenomenon of 'temping'

Agency workers and their close equivalents form a very transient population. They tend to move very easily between agencies, in and out of temporary work and in and out of the labour market. Manpower calculates that the average period for which a person works for it (presumably the average of all spells of employment) is four months, although it also points out that 'many "temporary" workers have been continuously employed by Manpower for several years and three and five year service awards for temporaries are a frequent occurrence' (Manpower, 1985). The short average duration of all spells of working with an agency is also consistent with the picture of a large number of persons working on this basis for very brief periods only. The FRES estimates that their members might have had about 60,000 temporaries on the payroll at any one time in 1985 (a figure broadly consistent with the LFS data), but that some half a million persons might have worked for an agency for some period in the course of that year (interview with FRES).

According to the Labour Force Survey, the proportion of agency workers working on a temporary basis because they do not want permanent jobs is considerably higher than the average for all temporary workers and that the proportion of agency secretarial/office workers doing so is still higher (see Table 5.1). The numerous surveys of (their own) 'temps' conducted by agencies supplying secretarial and office staff (see, for example, Alfred Marks, 1982; Reed, 1986; Manpower, 1986), whilst suffering from selectivity bias and/or containing leading questions, show that a substantial proportion of 'temps' are looking for permanent jobs; but they also suggest that some of these at least are using their experience of temporary jobs to find out what sort of permanent work they would like. Moreover, a similar or larger proportion claim either to enjoy the frequent change of tasks and environment, the flexibility of 'temping' and of being able to take spells off between assignments, or to have commitments which make continuous working impossible; even if, as one recent survey

(Manpower, 1986) showed, this was sometimes to be set off against a feeling of employment insecurity.

A feeling of employment insecurity might be thought to stem from the agency's lack of obligation to provide assignments on a continuous basis, and thus its inability to guarantee its workers a regular income. However, it should be asked how serious a problem is the lack of continuity of working. The large majority of agency workers are to be found in one region: 72 per cent are in Greater London and the South East, and in a very limited number of occupations - 45 per cent are in secretarial/office-type jobs [see Chapter 2] - and their services are greatly in demand. We have already referred to the competition between agencies to attract and retain them.[5] For such agency workers enforced breaks in working would be exceptional. In addition, the agencies themselves will be keen to make sure that they can offer follow-on assignments, since they are aware that they might otherwise lose their workers. Manpower, which operates a system of layoffs for staff to whom it cannot offer an assignment, estimated that between five and ten per cent of its workforce might be laid off at any one time. However, it made clear that it tried to keep the duration of such layoffs to a minimum, and suggested also that it was its industrial, not its secretarial/office staff, who were most likely to be affected by them (interview with Manpower).

The tight regional labour market for secretarial/office skills seems of itself to give rise to agency working. Employers' competition for scarce labour produces a high turnover of staff. This creates temporary vacancies which then have to be filled. The need to fill these vacancies quickly means that an agency is preferred to advertising and search, and in addition such a strategy avoids the administrative burden of taking persons on and off payroll whose stay will be limited. More important, people interested in temporary working are more likely to choose to be as agency workers rather than direct employees. One reason for this is that the agencies supply them efficiently with information about assignments. A second is that the agencies' rates of pay are often higher than those of the client organisations.

Pay rates for agency secretarial/office staff are determined very much by market forces and, particularly in Greater London and the South East, might as a result be increased two or three times per year. On the other hand, pay rates for secretarial/office staff in client organisations are often bureaucratically determined and usually cannot be adjusted to take account of supply and demand without disturbing established relativities (see IDS, 1986b). When the hourly rates agency workers receive are compared with the notional hourly earnings of many regular staff, excluding the value of such fringe benefits as holiday and sick pay and pensions (the so-called 'bottom-line comparison'), many 'temps' appear substantially better off than people in traditional employment. If the latter become aware of this, they too might be encouraged to switch to agency working. The shortage of regular staff is exacerbated and employers might begin to find that they are filling permanent positions on a temporary basis.

Where there is a shortage of labour in a regional or occupational labour market and pay scales are not sufficiently flexible to enable employers to respond to it, it may be only via the displacement of permanent staff by agency workers that the occupational labour market is able to find its equilibrium. Many agencies have tried to argue that using temporary workers can be cheaper than using permanent staff, because the employer pays only for the hours he needs and because the non-wage labour costs of agency workers are lower. However, a study commissioned by FRES, the primary objective of which was to give support to these claims, made very clear that for certain categories of worker, particularly secretarial/keyboard staff in central London and computer staff, agency supplied labour was more expensive (Rothwell/Mingard, 1985). This result provides important evidence in favour of the proposition that the remuneration of regular staff in these occupations and/or regions is below the market level.

Whilst much of our discussion has been conducted with reference to South Eastern secretarial/office staff, its substance holds for other regional/occupational labour markets too. Examples are health authorities 'being forced to pay huge sums to private locum agencies providing temporary medical cover as more doctors opt for higher private rates' and 'local councils ... paying £1,000 per week to specialist agencies to fill a single accountant's job' because they could not recruit permanent staff on the nationally agreed salary scales were reported recently (*The Times*, 24/11/86 and 5/9/7). In the following section we describe how the same forces are at work in the market for data processing staff, on which we focused most of our case studies of agency working.

Contract computer staff

As a relatively new and very fast growing sector, the information technology (IT) industry has, perhaps inevitably, suffered shortages of qualified labour (see Connor/Pearson, 1986; NCC, 1985). Symptoms of these shortages are very high levels of data processing (DP) staff turnover and substantial rates of increase in pay levels and in the value of fringe benefits. For specific skills, in particular regions and for particular employers, the shortage of labour can be severe. In the course of our case studies, we found that programmers/analysts capable of working in certain specific software/hardware areas (for example, IBM System 38, PICK) were extremely scarce, in some cases so much so that 'nobody is training them any more' (since high turnover rates meant they would not have the chance to amortise the training investment). We also found that in the South East of England (including Greater London), where the density of IT employers is very high, DP staff turnover levels as high as 40 per cent were being recorded in 1986,[6] compared to (only!) 25 per cent in the previous year (quoted in *Computing*, 30/10/86). In the rest of the country, where the density of IT employers is much lower, turnover was much lower, perhaps in the order of 10 per cent and often less.

Finally, we found that organisations outside the computing services industry tend to experience higher DP staff turnover than those within it. Computing services industry employers have very flexible salary systems which make it much easier to pay the rate the market requires for skills in question. Those outside it have salary systems tied to those for the industry in which they are operating. If that industry is not expanding, as the computing services industry is, its overall salary levels, and hence those of DP staff, are likely to be below those obtaining in computing services. Employers in public administration and in traditional production and service organisations have been attempting to restructure their salary systems or to add special supplements in an attempt to attract and retain DP staff (see IDS, 1986c), but such adjustments cannot be made easily. They risk pressures to 'follow on' from non-DP staff and their representatives and might, as a consequence, be inadequate to meet their intended objectives.

The inability to compete on salary terms, which creates staff shortages for certain organisations, is compounded in many cases by an inability to offer sufficiently satisfying work to attract labour with the skills that are desired. Organisations with established DP departments require staff who are able to take on software 'development' work (modifying, adding to, or creating new software systems) as required, but who, in the interim, will also undertake 'maintenance' work (keeping the system running). Such maintenance work is, however, not considered sufficiently interesting or challenging by many of those who are qualified to do development work. Quite apart from the immediate salary, they are not prepared to stay in position once the development tasks have been completed. In a fast moving industry they fear that, unless they are continuously involved in development work, their skills will deteriorate, and this will affect not only their future earning power, but also their ability to take on the sort of work they enjoy.

The processes we described for secretarial/office staff in the previous section are thus likely to be at work. The high level of turnover creates vacancies that need to be filled on an interim basis. The inflexibility of certain salary systems means that permanent positions can only be filled on a temporary basis. What might initially have been envisaged as a permanent position is broken down into its component parts. In the case of the example in the preceding paragraph, the maintenance function remains performed by permanent staff but the development function is now performed by temporary staff brought in via an agency. And in such a situation it becomes difficult to say whether the temporary worker is brought in because of a shortage of permanent staff or because there is (now) a once-off task to be performed.

Moreover, once such a situation arises, it has its own repercussions. We have already referred to the 'bottom line' calculations made by people working alongside agency 'temps'; these were continually mentioned by users and suppliers of contract computer staff too. Many sought, by no means always successfully, to avoid using temporary staff for precisely this reason. In addition, it was suggested that the inability of certain non-computing services industry organisations to attract sufficiently qualified staff to run their DP departments was leading to the operation of that whole department being contracted out. The physical equipment remained on site but the operating staff was provided by an external organisation, via a so-called 'FM deal' (facilities maintenance deal). The organisation having the contract is able to man up more successfully since it has its own, independent and higher salary levels[7] and, by having a number of such contracts and also being involved in other (development) work for other clients, it can continue to offer its staff a sufficient variety of tasks.

The special characteristics of contract computer staff.

If there are the same pressures contributing to the use of contract computer staff as for agency secretarial/office staff, the two groups are in other ways very different. Agency secretarial/office staff are almost exclusively female, contract computing staff almost exclusively male. Moreover, whilst the first group usually have only intermediate level qualifications and are performing non-executive, non-developmental tasks, the second have higher level qualifications and perform developmental and even managerial tasks. As well as programmers and analysts, agencies supply team leaders and project managers who oversee groups of programming and analysis staff. Although these people will normally be leading/managing other contractors, not regular employees, it is unusual to find any agency secretarial/office staff who have a supervisory function.[8] In addition, the assignments on which contract computing staff operate are of much longer duration. Most placements of agency secretarial/office staff are for a period as short as two weeks or less, albeit subject to extension, but the assignments advertised for computer staff are of three months, or more often six months and sometimes one year or even two year duration, again subject to extension.

Finally, the manner of remuneration and, more important, the de jure employment status of contract computer staff tend to differ from agency secretarial/office staff. Both are paid according to hours booked, but, as we pointed out earlier, there is an increasing tendency for the big agencies to offer secretarial/office staff such fringe benefits as sickness and holiday pay. For computer staff this did not appear to be so. We encountered one agency offering (free) training to its contractors via a system of credit points acquired through service, but it seems this practice is unusual. Computer staff agencies might seek to maintain contractors' loyalty, but more by keeping them supplied with assignments than by offering them employee-like benefits. Rather the image of self-employment is promoted. For some, perhaps still the majority of contractors the agency deducts tax at source and pays Class I (dependent employee's) social security contributions. However, while an important proportion of agency-supplied computer staff are self-employed, only a few agency secretarial/office workers are. Moreover, most self-employed contract computer staff are self-employed not only in the sense of being responsible for their own tax and paying Class II (self-employed person's) social security contributions, but also in the sense of being one-man, limited companies.

Incorporation has an appeal because of the image the person concerned can present 'I'm the director of my own company/I run a consultancy'. It also has substantial material advantages - the ability to raise loans is greater, the opportunity for setting off and writing off business expenses are more generous and, because tax to be paid at the end of any one financial year is assessed in relation to the previous year's results, organisations with a growing turnover have a lower effective tax rate than they would if tax were assessed on current activities. The nature of contract computer staff jobs imposes substantially heavier work-related expenses upon them than upon agency secretarial/office staff. They usually have their own personal computers, they need to subscribe to technical journals and pay for (relatively expensive) training and familiarisation courses in order to update their skills, their work tends to be spread over a wider geographical area and the need for a car is greater. However, the standing of their occupations - the fact that a programmer or analyst is regarded as a 'professional' in a way in which a typist or word processor operator is not, also makes it easier for them to acquire self-employed status. The tax and social security authorities are less likely to consider that the motive for doing so is avoidance. In addition, contract computer staff often gain advice and assistance from the agencies through which they work on how to proceed with incorporation, and are often encouraged by them to take this step.

Contracting as permanent employment

The fact that many contract computer staff incorporate themselves as one-man companies suggests that to describe them as temporary workers is in some ways misleading. The existence of the company suggests a permanence of operations that transcends the temporariness of any of the individual assignments the contractor himself undertakes. Many companies or enterprises, no matter what they produce, are engaged in the satisfaction of a series of customer orders. An order is not for ever: it is fulfilled and new orders have to be gained. However, the business of producing is, or is hoped to be, permanent. The difference between a more conventional company and an incorporated contract computer programmer/analyst is merely that the former can and does respond simultaneously to a multiplicity of orders which partly overlap and partly succeed one another. As a consequence, although a company might have more or less orders at any one time, it is less likely to be without any orders than the one-man operation which can contract to only one customer at any one time. Nevertheless, as was also suggested with respect to South Eastern secretarial/office staff, there is the opportunity for computer staff to make a (semi-)permanent career out of 'temping', and with the latter group this is made more explicit by the creation of the (semi-)permanent entity of the company. On the other hand, the effective independence of the individual contract programmer or analyst is not thereby enhanced, and he remains as dependent as the temporary secretary or typist upon intermediaries (the agencies) to provide a flow of work.

Contracting as precarious employment

If for many contract computer staff their employment is more permanent than temporary, it is also pertinent to ask whether it is more safe than precarious. We have already indicated that the incidence of 'involuntary' temporary working is lower amongst agency workers than amongst all temporary workers. Our impression is that almost all contract computer staff are voluntarily working on this basis. Because they have skills for which there is an excess demand, their security, not in an individual assignment but of being able to earn, is relatively great. Equally their earnings are high. For these reasons, and not only because their place of work is constantly changing, hardly any contract computer staff are organised into trade unions. Most feel, perhaps rightly, that they have little or no need for them, that they are able to and indeed profit from individualism. The same is likely to be true for South Eastern secretarial/office staff, and throws into question the chances of success of campaigns to recruit them such as recently initiated by the major Transport and General Workers Union (TGWU) (see *Financial Times*, 5 and 6/12/86).

However, the ability of contract computer staff to dispense with trade unions to further their interests is enhanced by a number of additional factors. First, the population of contract computer staff is much smaller than that of agency secretarial/office workers and, insofar as there are fewer people working on this basis for a very short term or occasional basis, has a much higher stability of membership. Second, as well as being rather homogeneous with respect to age, contract computer staff share an exclusive body of technical knowledge and this, despite their individualism, promotes a sense of common identity. Third, and as a consequence of the last two factors, they have been able to develop a number of networks, more or less formal, through which they can contact one another. These range from telephone calls between acquaintances and friends to meetings at training/familiarisation courses, and from participation in the affairs of independent computing associations to communicating through the columns of their own specialist fortnightly journal (the *Freelance Informer*). Since all of these channels permit information to circulate rapidly, contract computer staff are well equipped to protect themselves from becoming involved with, or exploited by, unscrupulous agencies or client organisations.

If trade unions are to have any success in organising contract computer staff it might be by the provision of non-traditional membership services. The General and Municipal union's white collar section (MATSA) has started an experimental recruitment campaign aimed not just at 'non-standard' workers who are part-time and temporary but also at the self-employed. One of the services it is offering to attract the self-employed is an introduction to financial and legal consultants who are prepared to offer union members especially favourable fees for their advice (see *Financial Times*, 31/3/87 and 30/4/87). Precisely these services might be attractive or useful to the one-man companies through which contract computer staff operate.

Conclusions

The legal status of agency workers is at first sight rather anomalous. Under tax and social security law they are normally regarded as dependent employees, but under labour law most are regarded as self-employed. Only those whose services are supplied by organisations which operate as 'works contractors' are dependent employees. However, the distinction between such organisations and most 'agencies' is an unclear one. Moreover, whilst many agencies now seek to make clear that the relationship with their temporary workers is not one of employment, many of the larger ones also offer them 'employee-like' fringe benefits and try to encourage agency loyalty. On the other hand, it might not be very important for most agency workers what their employment status is. Many do not remain sufficiently long as temporary workers or with any one agency to be entitled to any rights even if they were to have dependent employee status. This transience is largely a consequence of their own choice and wishes rather than something forced upon them. Indeed, as a result of an excess demand for their skills, enforced breaks in working are rare. What is more, because the earnings they thereby achieve can be higher than those of regular employees, some people choose to work on a temporary rather than a permanent basis.[9]

It appears that the use of agency working is greatest in cases in which there are severe occupational/regional labour shortages and where salary scales, because of the need to respect established differentials, cannot be adjusted upwards. This can be seen by reference to the labour market for secretarial/office skills in the South East and Greater London. Agency working might provide one means whereby this labour market can move towards equilibrium. Similarly, the use of contractors is sometimes the only way in which certain organisations can meet their demands for key computing skills.

Contract computer staff are also interesting because they differ from the traditional 'temp' secretary. They are men rather than women, they are more highly qualified, their assignments are longer and, most significantly, they are often very explicitly self-employed, operating as one-man limited companies. The nature of their jobs and the extent of work-related expenses means that incorporation has considerable material advantages for contract computer staff, as well as appealing to their sense of self-esteem as 'professionals'. However, the existence of the limited company underlines the (semi-)permanence of the individual's temporary working. Although any one assignment which the company has is of short duration, the company itself continues in being, following up that assignment by another.

Finally, it seems that despite the absence of formal systems of regulation, contract computer staff are potentially well protected from the vagaries of unscrupulous clients or agencies. This is not only because they face a 'bull market' for their skills, but also because they are a small and homogeneous population. Opportunities for informal contacts and the exchange of information and experiences are, in consequence, extensive, and they probably serve the individualistic-minded members of this particular labour force as a more than satisfactory substitute for trade unions. Although they are a larger and less tightly-knit group, this might well also apply to agency secretarial workers. Attempts by trade unions to organise such temporary workers might well make little headway, as much because the latter do not perceive that they need unions to protect them as because they are a transient population.

Whilst 'non-standard', agency working can scarcely be described as 'precarious' for the majority of office/secretarial workers or for contract computer staff. Because of the characteristics of the occupational and regional labour markets in which they operate, both these sorts of agency workers are likely to enjoy a higher degree of employment security than many members of the 'standard' labour force.

Notes

1.   The 1973 Act uses the term 'employment agency' to refer to a 'business ... providing services ... for the purpose of finding

workers employment with employers or of supplying employers with workers for employment by them' (S.13(2)), in other words, to refer to private placement bureaux. Many 'employment agencies' are simultaneously 'employment businesses', in fact their activities are sometimes difficult to distinguish. It is their opposition to private placement bureau, which they see as undermining the public employment service, which has been the main explanation for trade union hostility to agency working and, until recently, for their reluctance to recruit or organise agency workers (on this last see Towers/Harrison 1981).

2. Leighton (1986) argues that although there is no obligation to offer an agency worker an assignment, once the agency has done so, and the offer has been accepted, an employment relationship exists for the duration of that assignment. She also argues that, if an agency does not exercise detailed control, it nevertheless exercises the ultimate control of the worker, since it can withdraw him or refuse to offer him another assignment should his performance fail to meet required standards.

3. Another major agency, Brook Street Bureau, has recently offered employee status and the guarantee of work to certain of its temporary office workers, those with 'top skills, wide experience and who have been with the agency for at least three months' (see *Financial Times*, 12/4/88).

4. The parallel with developments in the documentation of casual workers' conditions of engagement [see Chapter 6] are to be noted.

5. 'Competition is intense. There is a shortage of good temps, particularly in London. Several thousand bookings go unfilled every week'. Dinah Cornish, Managing Director of Brook Street Bureau, quoted in Cunningham, 1987.

6. This was attributed to the demand for DP staff induced by 'Big Bang' - the deregulation of many of the City's financial activities and the major extension of computer-based trading.

7. The parallels with and the differences from the sub-contracting of catering and cleaning services in both the public and private

sectors should be noted. In these cases one of the objectives is often to enable *lower* rates of pay and/or fringe benefits to be paid than if the workers concerned were remunerated on scales applying to the organisation itself.

8. The LFS records no agency workers amongst the (KOS) occupational group of *supervisors* of typists, office machine operators, telephonists, etc.

9. The entrepreneurial characteristics of agency workers, and the regional/occupational labour market conditions which encourage agency working as an institution, can be likened to the entrepreneurial characteristics of self-employed, or labour only, subcontracting, building workers, and the regional/occupational labour market conditions which encouraged the growth of labour only subcontracting in the building industry in the late 1950s and early 1960s (see Phelps Brown, 1968). I am grateful to Steve Evans of Warwick University for pointing this out.

Table 5.1   Reason for taking temporary employment given by agency workers

Percentages

	Job incs. training	Couldn't find perm. job	Didn't want perm. job	Other/ no answer	(n) 000s
all temporary workers	5.2	35.6	27.1	32.1	(1,493)
all agency workers	0.6	33.2	39.4	26.8	(50)
agency secretarial/ office workers	1.4	35.8	52.2	10.6	(23)

* Clerks, secretaries, shorthand typists, receptionists; office-machine operators; telephonists radio and telegraph operators (see Chapter 2, Table 2.5).

Source: 1984 LFS

6 Casual working

The term 'casual working' frequently conjures up suggestions of 'pre-industrial' or 'Victorian' employment practices alien to those thought prevailing in an advanced welfare society. It implies a process of hiring and firing by the day or by the hour and a high level of job insecurity. The industrial relations problems of the docks in the 1950s and 1960s could, in the eyes of many commentators, be ascribed to the institution of casual working and the (ultimately successful) attempts by the trade unions to replace it with a system of regular employment for dock labourers (see Wilson, 1972). Equally, in much present day socio-legal writing (for example, Deakin, 1986), casual working is discussed as an example of 'precarious' employment. It is generally recognised that casual working is still important in certain industrial/occupational labour markets, particularly that of the hotels and catering industry, although the question of whether the casual status of their jobs is a source of disadvantage to the people who work in this fashion is one which has, as yet, scarcely been answered.

In this chapter we consider of casual working in the hotels and catering sector. We sketch briefly the legal definition of casual working and go on to consider the special features of certain business operations within the hotels and catering industry which explain why casual workers are to be found there. Next we look at the characteristics of the casual labour force, and we conclude by considering the relevance of their lack of coverage by the principal provisions of employment protection legislation.

What makes a casual worker 'casual'?

The (now superseded) Wages Council order for the licensed residential establishments industry described a casual worker as one 'who undertakes engagements on either an hourly or day-to-day basis ... ' However, it is not only the extreme temporariness of his engagement which distinguishes the casual worker from other temporary workers, but also his or her employment status. The Wages Council order continued '... and has the right to choose, without penalty, whether or not to come to work', and, according to current interpretations of labour law, this means that casual workers are not employees at all. Rather, they are a form of self-employed person, contracting to supply their services to client organisations. The organisation engaging the casual worker is not obliged to offer him any work. Equally, if it does offer him work, he is not obliged to accept it. This 'lack of mutual obligation' is the key factor arguing against the existence of a conventional employer/employee relationship.

Another distinguishing feature of casual working, and one likely to influence courts in their conclusion that it is a form of self-employment, is the exclusion of the worker from access to fringe benefits. Casual workers are rarely paid when absent because of sickness, nor are they normally entitled to paid holidays or other paid time off. Moreover, their pay is not always subject to tax and social insurance deductions.

In the course of our case studies in the manufacturing sector we encountered several organisations which had recently introduced or extended their use of temporary working and which referred to the workers concerned as 'casuals'. Equally, it is not uncommon to find such introductions or extensions of temporary working labelled by those who are critical of them as the introduction or extension of 'casualisation' (see, for instance, the report of a motion passed at the 1986 conference of the engineering workers union (AUEW) which 'attacked the greater use of casual workers by employers' in *Financial Times*, 23/4/86). However, in nearly all the instances of so-called casual working in manufacturing examined, it is doubtful if the term 'casual' was applied correctly. Most of the workers concerned had or would have been deemed by the courts to have had contracts of employment. Most employers accepted statutory notice requirements, and most accorded the workers at least a minimal entitlement to fringe benefits. Others made commitments to offer their 'casuals' a minimum level of work, which made the relationship inconsistent with one based upon an absence of obligation. It was only in the hotels and catering industry that we encountered a widespread use of temporary working which was not only called casual working by the parties concerned but which also was likely to be, or had been, unequivocally accepted as such by labour courts.

Casual working in hotels and catering

Within the hotels and catering sector, casual labour is used predominantly by organisations engaged in what is termed 'functional catering'. This last is not the day-to-day catering provided by a commercial restaurant, a hotel dining room or a canteen, but catering at one-off 'events'. Examples of such 'events' are special lunches, dinners or banquets, sporting or cultural occasions, conferences and exhibitions. Most 'events' are of a very short duration - in the case of a banquet a matter of a few hours - but some can last longer - in the case of certain sporting events, conferences or exhibitions several days, or even one or two weeks. Any one 'event' is likely to be on a different scale from the one preceding or succeeding it and there are likely to be gaps between events. Where 'events' last several days, the level of activity can vary from day to day, sometimes in a predictable sometimes an unpredictable fashion. First and last days might be busy; the weather might have an important influence upon attendance. Often a seasonal factor intervenes, so that there is a banqueting season (the winter months), a conference season (the autumn months), an exhibition season (the winter months) and a sporting season (the summer months). For some organisations specialising in catering for certain kinds of 'event', or for some operating in certain regions, these seasons are more pronounced than for others. For example, the banqueting season is much shorter in the provinces than in London.

The basic or 'core' labour forces employed by organisations undertaking functional catering is likely to be small. In many cases it consists of no more than a few managers/supervisors. Additional labour is brought in as and when required, and is brought in almost exclusively on a casual basis. Some organisations that face a pronounced seasonal pattern in their activities (for example, those whose activities included the provision of catering facilities at summer sporting events) supplement this managerial supervisory core with other staff hired on a seasonal basis [see Chapter 7 below], but this practice is relatively unusual. Moreover, it affects only certain types of staff, primarily lower level managers and supervisors, occasionally also skilled chefs. On the other hand, even when there is a practically continuous, minimal level of activity throughout a season or year, semi-skilled and unskilled positions are always filled by casuals.

In addition to using casual workers to man up for 'events', we also found cases of organisations bringing them in to cope with peaks in what might be termed their 'more continuous' activities. One example is the practice of engaging casual chambermaids, porters, waiters, bar and kitchen staff to cover the traditionally busy week or two around Christmas, or to help out at other times of the year when hotel occupancy rates exceed expected levels. Another is the use of casuals to supplement the basic staff in a restaurant or bar on busy days or at busy times of the year. Casuals might also be engaged to fill temporary vacancies caused by the departure or absence of regular staff members. However, longer term temporary labour requirements, such as those experienced over summer by hotels at holiday resorts, are usually met by the recruitment of seasonal workers.

Managing casual labour

Most organisations involved in functional catering establish and maintain lists of people whom they have screened for their suitability and who have declared themselves available for casual work. In small organisations such lists are managed on an informal basis, in large on a much more formal basis. More important, however, the large organisations with which we had contact had all sought to make very clear the precise status of their casual staff. The terms and conditions of their engagement (and many organisations are careful not to use the word 'employment') are set out in special handbooks, or in the contracts which casual workers are required to sign, and these seek to make the parties' lack of mutual obligation clear. Clauses such as the following are typical:

No contractual relationship whatsoever shall exist between the Company and the casual worker covered by its terms and conditions on any day when the casual worker does not attend for work with the Company. You are entitled to choose whether or not to accept engagements which may be offered to you either on an hourly or sessional basis but the Company does not guarantee continuous employment and nor is the Company under any obligation to offer further engagements or re-engagements. Any engagement of casual work does not constitute a contract of employment between the casual worker and the Company.

At the same time, these large organisations are equally scrupulous in ensuring that tax and social security deductions are made for their casual workers. The tax and social security authorities regard casual workers as dependent employees and normally insist upon deduction of payments and contributions at source. Recognising that this stands in contradiction to the statements contained in the terms and conditions of engagement which they offer their casual workers, some organisations seek to make it clear that they are no more than 'collecting agents for the revenue'. Nevertheless, they require their casual workers to furnish them with appropriate identification and evidence of their tax status. Only in the case of engagements lasting for a single day or less, and involving people with whom the organisation does not expect to have further contact in the near future, might payment be made without any deductions. When this happens the organisation will insist upon the workers concerned signing a document acknowledging their own responsibility for tax.

If, for employment law purposes, large organisations are anxious to stress that the parties have no obligations to one another, they are also keen to ensure that the situation is not one of anarchy. Although they face daily and substantial fluctuations in demand for their output, they wish to ensure that they do have sufficient staff available to help them satisfy this demand. Thus it is important for them that commitments to work, once they are given, are honoured. A casual worker who, without good reason, fails to turn up for an assignment which he has accepted is unlikely to be offered assignments in the future. Refusal of an assignment does not normally result in any disadvantage to the casual worker, but frequent refusals, even with good reason, are likely to diminish his chances of having offers made since they put his availability into question.

Where 'events' last longer than a few hours or one day, the need for order in the relationship is increased. Unless certain peaks are foreseen, the engagements offered are not for the day but for the full length of the 'event'. If the casual worker cannot make himself available for the full length of time requested, he is unlikely to be offered the assignment, although exceptions will be made if the organisation is facing a tight labour market and can only cover its manpower requirements by bringing in 'part-timers'. On the other hand, the organisation will always retain the right to terminate the engagement prematurely if it considers this may be necessary. Most casual workers are paid by the day or hour, and this alone determines the notice they must be given. Such flexibility of disposition has substantial advantages: it means, for example, that if a sporting event ends prematurely because of bad weather, or if attendance falls short of anticipated levels, some or all of the casual labour force can be discharged and workers need not be carried when there is nothing for them to do. However, when there is no chance that demand will fluctuate over the duration of the 'event', for example where the 'event' is the week or two of heavy bookings at a hotel over Christmas, payment might be offered in the form of a lump sum at the end and might include a 'loyalty bonus' for those who stay for the full period.

The casual labour force

The casual labour force in the hotels and catering industry is not a homogeneous one. We can identify three categories of casual worker, each having very different characteristics. First, there is the most peripheral category, composed of persons to whom the user organisation has the lowest degree of commitment. Such workers are normally used for the most unskilled tasks; insofar as they receive any training, it is brief. They tend to undertake such jobs as simple bar work, portering, the preparation and serving of 'fast food' and washing-up. Their relationship with the organisation is likely to be transient; they are brought in for a particular event and might or might not work again for the same organisation.

Second, there is a category composed of people who work on an irregular basis, but with whom the organisation is interested in developing a continuing relationship. They are likely to be used in relatively more skilled positions and those which require an element of 'representativeness', such as 'silver service' waiting. A number of organisations to which we spoke provided (paid) training for people filling such positions, despite the fact that they would only be working for them on a casual basis and might even use the skills they acquired working for other organisations. We found these casual workers given such names as 'bank staff', and they would be the first people to whom the organisation would turn when it needed to bring in extra workers. Sometimes the relationship between the organisation and the worker extended over many years. Some of these casual workers possess the additional advantage of having contacts amongst other persons interested in occasional work, so that they rather than all of these individuals are contacted when a large number of staff are required.[1]

Third, there is the category of person with whom the organisation has an exclusive and effectively full-time relationship. These persons are frequently referred to as 'regular casuals', although the term is also sometimes used to refer to people in the second category. They tend to hold the most highly skilled and responsible positions, such as head waiter or wine butler, and to be found in organisations with a substantial volume of banqueting activities. Not only do they receive the first offers of any work that is available (and in other than special circumstances always accept such offers), but also the organisations for which they work undertake a sufficient volume of business to make offers of work for many days each week and for most weeks of the year. They are likely to stay for a long time with one organisation, and indeed many organisations seek to bind them to them by offering fringe benefits, particularly in the form of 'loyalty bonuses' to encourage them to return at the start of each new banqueting season.

As well as taking, as in the preceding paragraphs, an employer's perspective of the casual labour force, we can examine it in terms of the labour market situation and interests of the casual workers themselves. Many of them, it was suggested by the organisations we spoke to, are married women with domestic commitments who are unable or unwilling to work on a regular basis but who value the opportunity to take on occasional work outside normal hours, particularly in the pre-Christmas period (the height of the banqueting season). Some are retirees who want a part-time job. Others are students who seek work during vacations or at weekends and yet others are students on hotel and catering courses who are picking up practical experience. Several organisations pointed out how, for certain large events, they made arrangements with local colleges which run such courses to offer work during term time that could be integrated into the teaching programme.

A second group is made up of people who work, or who could work if they chose to, almost full-time and full-year-round in the industry. These people were largely to be found in the more skilled positions described above. Some of them work for a number of different organisations, and some of this sub-group operate via specialist employment agencies, which act as intermediaries between them and the user organisation. More interesting is the sub-group of people who not only work full-time and full-year but also exclusively for one organisation. Perhaps the most important thing to be remarked about them is that their numbers are very small and that almost all of them are men. Moreover, they are concentrated in a very few geographic locations. Most are working in central London, some also in one or two other major cities, since it is only there that the sort of prestigious hotels and banqueting suites which can mount an almost unbroken series of events are to be found. Such people, we would suggest, are also 'voluntary' temporary workers. Their often very high and frequently untaxed earnings from gratuities at the large and lavish events at which they serve more than make up for the low basic rates they are paid, the absence of substantial fringe benefits and the existence of a short off-season in which they cannot earn.

A third group consists of unemployed people who take casual jobs in catering for want of any alternative. The importance of this group in any one organisation's casual labour force depends largely on the state of the local labour market. Thus in Greater London and the South East, where unemployment is relatively low, it is lower (and, indeed, to man-up for some events several organisations find it necessary to bus people in from other parts of the country), whilst in certain northern conurbations, where unemployment is high, it rises correspondingly. It also varies with the category of job or occupation. More skilled jobs are not usually undertaken by the otherwise unemployed, who are mainly to be found in low-skilled jobs. It should also be noted that many of the otherwise unemployed have little sense of attachment to the organisation for which they work and regard the jobs they have as transitory. Thus, one large contract caterer in a northern city with a high unemployment rate, whose casuals consisted almost entirely of otherwise unemployed people, estimated that as many as four times the number of people passed through its list of those available for casual work in the course of a year than were on that list at any one point in time.

With the aid of the LFS we were able to examine further the extent to which members of the temporary labour force in the hotel and catering industry were working on that basis because they had been unable to find permanent jobs, and to what extent they were doing so because they did not want permanent jobs. As well as giving us data for the industry, the LFS provided us with information about the narrow (KOS) occupational group of waiters and bar staff in which casuals are concentrated. As Table 6.1 below shows, the proportion of temporary hotel and catering staff who can be described as working on that basis 'involuntarily' is lower, and the proportion who can be classified as working on that basis 'voluntarily' is higher than for the generality of the temporary labour force.

The appropriateness of increased employment protection

In an important way casual working demands the same disciplines of the worker as more traditional working. A traditional worker who absents himself without good reason or who persistently fails to show up for his job is likely to be disciplined or dismissed, and a casual worker who fails to appear without being able to offer good justification, or who is seldom available, is likely to be dropped from the list of those who an organisation will contact. In particular, to be a 'regular casual' working more or less continuously for one organisation is incompatible with working only as and when one chooses. Such 'regular casuals' can remain 'regular casuals' only if they are prepared to accept the schedules set for them and to take their free days when there are no events and their holidays during the off-season.

Indeed, the most frequently cited judicial ruling on the employment law status of casual workers (the 'O'Kelly case', see Leighton 1984), concerned precisely this last category of people - a group of 'regular casuals' at a major London hotel who sought redress for being dismissed following their efforts to secure trade union recognition. The court held that the practice of making first offers of work to a selected group of people who had declared themselves available, and the practice of declaring oneself available to ensure that such offers would be made, whilst an arrangement 'of mutual advantage' to the parties, was not one involving contractual commitments or mutual obligation. Equally, it did not find the hotel's practice of sanctioning certain refusals of offers of work by the temporary suspension of further offers to be inimical to the absence of an employment relationship. Instead, it viewed it merely as the reflection of 'an inequality of economic power' between the parties. Whilst this decision has been criticised as a 'narrow' interpretation of the law (*ibid*)[2], our examination of the nature of casual working and the characteristics of the casual labour force in the hotels and catering sector raises the question of whether according casual workers employee status, and thus bringing them within the coverage of employment protection legislation, would be of any great relevance.

First, we should remember that the individual assignments for which casual workers are engaged are all of a short duration. They might on occasion last several days rather than one day or less, but we seldom heard of them lasting longer than two weeks or so. Indeed, where there were longer 'events', these were normally staffed with seasonal workers employed on very different terms and conditions. As we have seen in Chapter 1, most employment law rights are available only to people having a minimum of four weeks' service, whilst protection against unfair dismissal for other than trade union activities, even with the law at its most liberal, required six months' service. With respect to those casuals who worked for only one organisation, it might be argued that the actual employment relationship lasted longer than the individual assignment and that interruptions were the consequence of 'a shortage of work', but this would be difficult to sustain. For most of those concerned, the durations of the interruptions would be substantially in excess of the durations of the periods of working.

Second, any refusal of an offer of work because an engagement with another organisation had been accepted, although normally not sufficient to debar a casual from further offers, would constitute a break of employment. Equally, the right of casual workers with whom an organisation has a longer term relationship to be able to choose whether or not to work (even if this right cannot be abused) is incompatible with a contractual relationship which obliges work which is offered to be undertaken. Again, refusals of work which would be insufficient to prejudice the relationship between the casual worker and the organisation would nevertheless seem to imply a break in employment.

Third, those who do have long-term relationships with particular organisations, whether these relationships are exclusive or not, enjoy a considerable level of informal protection. They tend to have skills which are often not immediately available on the external labour market and their reliability and competence is not in question. Indeed, it is precisely for such reasons that organisations have sought to develop long-term relationships with them. This is all the more true of those casual workers who work on an almost full-time, full-year basis for a single organisation. They have skills and qualities which make them highly valuable and which most organisations regard as being in short supply. An arbitrary and unwarranted termination of their engagement would be against the organisation's own interests. Moreover, were it to occur, such workers should have little difficulty in finding a similar position elsewhere. This view was shared by the trade union officials to whom we spoke.

This is not to say that trade unions are not concerned about casual workers in the hotel and catering industry; they very much are and are very keen to increase their membership amongst them. The General and Municipal union (GMBATU) has its own Hotel and Catering Workers Union section, and it pursued the 'O'Kelly case' on behalf of the workers concerned. It has also sought to negotiate, and with some organisations managed to conclude, 'casual workers charters'. These give casual workers the right, if they feel that their employment has taken on a de facto regular status, to raise the matter with the organisation and request that their contractual relationship be revised accordingly (interview with GMBATU). The Transport and General Workers Union too has been active in the industry, and its latest recruitment drives is also aimed at casuals. The highly transient nature of the casual labour force in hotels and catering, and the low attachment to work of many casuals - itself often related to the fact that their jobs are very much part-time - mean that the unions' task will scarcely be an easy one. The chances of their initiative being successful, we suggest, have to be rated rather low.

Conclusions

Whilst many forms of temporary working have been pejoratively described as casual working, casual working is a special form of temporary working. It is characterised by very short durations of employment, in most cases by an exclusion of the worker concerned from all of the fringe benefits enjoyed many other workers, but above all by the categorization of the workers concerned as self-employed persons contracting to supply their services. According to decisions of labour courts, no legally enforceable relationship exists between the casual worker and the organisation for which he is working in the times when he is not engaged by them. There is no obligation to offer further work and no obligation to accept it. As a consequence, casual workers are not covered by employment protection legislation, and this in turn has led casual working to be described as 'precarious' employment in much socio-legal writing.

Our case studies of casual working were carried out in the hotels and catering industry where a large proportion of the casual labour force is to be found. Within that industry casual working is used primarily by organisations undertaking 'functional catering'. The very short duration of most of the 'events' for which they are providing services, and the gaps which occur between these 'events', make it highly appropriate for such organisations to bring in labour on a casual basis. Moreover, despite the apparent contradiction, casual working at least in this sector is a highly formalised system of working. This is particularly so in the large organisations with which we had contact. Formalisation goes beyond the clear documentation of casual status, to include the building up of lists of people who are available for such work and the provision of training for certain skills, particularly higher grade 'waiting' skills. In some cases long-term relationships grow up between casual workers and particular organisations. In a few cases, particularly in the banqueting establishments of a few large London hotels, where there is at least one 'event' on most days of the week and most weeks of the year, there are some casuals who work effectively full-time for the organisation concerned.

In lower-skilled and unskilled jobs, and in areas of higher unemployment, the casual labour force in hotels and catering includes people working on this basis because they are unable to find any other job. However, all the indications are that the majority of casual workers in hotels and catering are 'voluntary' casual workers. Many are married women who are interested only in occasional work, some are retired persons and some are students, of whom many are on catering courses and seeking practical experience. A small number of people, mostly skilled waiters/waitresses, are attracted to 'functional catering' work by the high gratuities they can earn. Again, they are mainly to be found in London, and because there is a high demand for their skills, they can be confident of a steady supply of engagements. A few of them can afford to rely upon a single organisation to offer them work throughout the year.

Repeated non-availability or failures to show up after agreeing to an engagement are likely to result in a discontinuation of offers of work, and in this sense casual working requires an acceptance of many of the same disciplines as apply to working in a regular fashion. This is especially so for people who work on a continuous basis as casual workers. As far as those who not only do this but also work exclusively for a single organisation are concerned, it makes the distinction between them and the regular employees of that organisation an unclear and almost unreal one. This raises the question of whether casual workers should not after all be allowed to enjoy the coverage of employment protection legislation. However, simply to accord casual workers a dependent employee status would be of little relevance to them. The engagements most undertake are so short and so intermittent that they would not acquire sufficient service to gain any substantial employment rights. On the other hand, those casual workers who manage to build up sufficent service are highly-skilled and have skills which are in short supply. An organisation would be most unlikely to dismiss them without good reason, and if it were to they would have little difficulty finding alternative work.

The employment of the otherwise unemployed members of the hotels and catering casual labour force is clearly precarious, but its precariousness scarcely stems from any inadequacies of employment protection legislation. The employment prospects of those who are voluntary casuals and who seek only occasional work is usually secured by the networks of reciprocity linking them to the organisations which have such work to offer. Finally, the full-time, full-year casual workers who most closely resemble regular employees have little need of employment protection legislation. The skills they possess make them a valued commodity which most organisations would be loath to lose and keen to gain.

Notes

1. These 'bookers', as they are often referred to, operate as a sort of informal agency. The persons whom they bring with them, however, are paid directly by the user organisation and not through them. 'Bookers' might receive a small sum per worker supplied, or a slightly higher hourly rate or an occasional small gratuity in return for their services.

2. It can also be suggested that it was contradicted by another case heard shortly afterwards but which concerned homeworkers not casual workers (the 'Gardiner and Taverna case') which was resolved very differently. The homeworkers' expectations that they would receive work regularly, and their effective inability to refuse consignments of work, meant that their situation was similar to that of the regular casuals in the 'O'Kelly case'. However, on this occasion the court concluded there did indeed exist an irreducable minimum of obligation sufficient to confer employee status (see Leighton, 1986). In fact, one year later another 'regular casual' employed by another large London hotel was held by the courts to be an employee, with the 'Gardiner and Taverna' ruling being used as justification for this decision. The minute

differences of circumstances between this, the 'Hamarat case', and the 'O'Kelly case' were commented upon by the court. The judgement led one observer to point out ruefully that there now existed a situation where two tribunals faced with similar circumstances could quite reasonably come to different conclusions, and that their rulings could not be overturned on appeal in the interests of consistency (IRS, 1985a).

Table 6.1   Reasons for taking temporary employment given by hotel and catering staff

Percentages

	Job includes training	Could not find perm. job	Did not find perm. job	Other/ no answer	(n) 000s
all temporary workers	5.2	35.6	27.1	32.1	(1,493)
hotels and catering industry	6.1	24.9	41.2	27.8	(127)
waiters and bar staff	-	23.6	45.6	30.8	(54)

Source: 1984 LFS

7 Short-term contract working

Most of the reasons why employers to bring in temporary workers are straightforward. They do so to replace people who are off on longer term absences, to undertake special one-off jobs, to provide extra cover during holiday periods and to meet seasonal demands for output. In some instances they might use agency workers - particularly when office skills are sought - or casual workers - particularly when the tasks are of short duration.[1] In the main, however, they employ their temporary workers directly and issue them with some sort of employment contract. We refer to such temporary workers as short-term contract workers and to such temporary working as short-term contract working.

In this chapter we examine a number of different forms of short-term contract working in a number of different sectors. We commence with the service sector, looking particularly at retailing and at the holiday and entertainments (night clubs, dance halls) industry. Here we consider short-term contract working in its most traditional form. In the second part of the chapter we concentrate on manufacturing industry, reporting on the experiences of a number of organisations which have only recently started to make use of temporary workers, and their reasons for doing so. Unlike the two preceding chapters we do not begin with a discussion of the labour law status of the workers concerned. This status is unambiguous and has not been the source of any judicial disputation. On the other hand, the nature of the contract of employment on which they are recruited can vary substantially and we describe the variations in some detail.

Traditional short-term contract working

The retailing, holidays and entertainments industries are industries which, it is widely recognised, experience seasonal peaks in the level of their activities. Seasonal peaks are not specific to the service sector; they are to be found in certain parts of manufacturing - particularly in food processing but also in a number of consumer goods industries - and in agriculture. Nevertheless, in terms of the numbers of temporary workers involved, the industries we consider are amongst the most important ones. This is not to say that they are homogeneous - the nature of the seasonal peaks, their duration and the kinds of people employed differ considerably.

The nature of seasonal work

Almost all large retailers face a Christmas peak lasting for a period of about two months and concentrated in the weeks before Christmas. The entertainments industry faces a similar peak of approximately the same duration and timing. Certain of the retailing organisations we spoke to mentioned a smaller, shorter peak at around Easter and many also hired temporary workers for a month or two over the summer to fill in for regular staff who were taking vacations. Those located at holiday resorts took on extra staff to deal with the increased demand brought about by an influx of summer visitors. The summer peak could last for several months, considerably longer than that at Christmas.

The same relatively long peak is, of course, to be found in the holiday industry itself. Our research here concentrated upon holiday camps, where most sites are open from May to September, providing a season lasting at least five months. In holiday camps the peaks were also of much greater magnitude than those in retailing and entertainment. Employers in these latter two sectors spoke of topping up their regular staff levels by perhaps some 10 per cent to cope with the Christmas peak. Holiday camps, on the other hand, employ only a very small number of permanent staff - mainly in managerial positions, to administer bookings and to undertake maintenance and cleaning - and might increase their labour forces almost tenfold by the height of the holiday season.

The positions into which seasonal workers are placed tend to be relatively unskilled ones demanding little or no previous experience. Most seasonal workers are given induction rather than training and are then placed in the lowest level jobs in the organisation. Regular staff, sometimes nominally of the same grade, provide a sort of supervision for them in the initial period and themselves tend to find that during the peak period they are doing, or doing more consistently, more responsible jobs than during the rest of the year. However, some on-the-job training, in skills such as cash handling or food preparation, is usually given to seasonal workers and this allows them to be moved into tasks which would have been denied them at the start of their employment.

In holiday camps seasonal workers are also found in more skilled and even supervisory positions. The manyfold increase in their staffing levels which the camps make effectively dictates this. Chefs, maintenance technicians and nurses are recruited on a seasonal basis. These people have acquired their skills elsewhere: they receive no training in the course of their seasonal employment and are assumed to be fully functional from their first day at work.

The seasonal labour force

In the same way that agency working attracts the 'agency worker' and casual working the 'casual worker', so too it seems does seasonal working attract the 'seasonal worker'. Many of those who take Christmas jobs in retail stores are, it was suggested, married women who are explicitly seeking a short-term job to help meet the extra expenses incurred at that time of the year. Some of them work regularly every Christmas, sometimes repeatedly with the same employer. Nearer to Christmas time they are supplemented by college and older school students, some of whom already work in the store on late night shopping evenings or at the weekend. Students also provide a substantial share of the summer staff taken on by holiday camps, at least for that part of the season which coincides with college vacations. In the entertainments industry one of the organisations to which we spoke pointed out that, precisely because the positions they are seeking to fill around Christmas are advertised as seasonal or temporary positions of a rather limited duration, they are normally filled by people with little interest in staying. In the holiday camps sector frequent reference was made to a category of 'persons who work in the holiday industry', by which was meant those who regularly spend the summer in jobs in camps and hotels and the winter in jobs abroad or on cruise ships. Such people, who can probably also be thought of as 'voluntary' temporary workers, often fill the more highly skilled and supervisory positions which the camps offer on a seasonal basis.

Otherwise unemployed people constitute an important seasonal labour force in the holiday camps sector. Nevertheless, the sort of jobs offered are really suitable only for those who can accept moving across the country and living in single person staff quarters for a prolonged period. Not surprisingly, the otherwise unemployed seasonal workers, like the rest of the camps' seasonal labour force, are mainly young - mostly in the 19 to 25 years age range. In areas of high unemployment there is an increase in the proportion of 'involuntary' temporary workers in the seasonal labour force in retailing. Organisations operating in the north of the country spoke of recruiting seasonal workers from amongst people who had contacted them looking for permanent positions. It should, however, be noted that seasonal jobs in retailing, like regular jobs in the sector, are predominantly part-time jobs. This, coupled with the fact that they are also relatively low paid, means that many of them are unattractive to many of the unemployed. Thus, even when they do provide employment to otherwise unemployed people, they do so primarily to unregistered part-time job seekers.

Recently a number of trade unions, especially the Transport and General (TGWU) and the General and Municipal (GMBATU) unions, have made efforts to increase their organisation of seasonal workers, just as the former has also made efforts to increase its organisation of agency workers [see Chapter 5]. The Transport and General Workers Union said it saw seasonal workers as potentially ripe for recruitment precisely because a considerable number returned to the same job year after year (see *Financial Times*, 7/1/87). On the other hand, even such seasonal workers' commitment to work, needs and interests are likely to be different from those of regular workers; this despite the fact that their pay or access to fringe benefits can be inferior to those of regular workers. Once again we must ask how successful the unions' recruitment campaigns will ultimately prove to be.

The terms and conditions of seasonal employment

Employers in all three sectors distinguish their seasonal workers from their regular workers in a number of ways. Most pay them on the same rates of pay, but because they lack seniority and are usually filling low-skilled, entry-level positions, seasonal workers' actual earnings are usually lower than those of comparable regular workers. In the holiday camps, seasonal workers are paid wages council (statutorily fixed) minimum rates whilst permanent staff are paid collectively agreed rates which are considerably higher. This practice is justified by reference to the fact that those permanent staff members performing notionally the same job take on a quasi-supervisory function during the peak period.

The principal differences with respect to conditions concern rights to fringe benefits. Either because they fail in any case to meet service requirements (often set at six months) or, where there are no service requirements because any 'temporary' employee is explicitly excluded, seasonal workers are not covered by company sick pay schemes designed to pay more than statutory benefits. Indeed, apart from workers in holiday camps who, because they are taken on for periods expected to be in excess of 13 weeks, qualify for statutory sickness pay, most seasonal workers are not entitled to any income replacement in case of absence.[2]

Staff whose employment is recognised as being temporary are also debarred from membership of any occupational pension schemes their employer operates, most of which are open only to workers who had satisfied a minimum service requirement - usually one year or more. In retailing temporary workers are often ineligible for staff discount schemes. Such practices are understandable: fringe benefits are seen as a reward for long-term commitment to the organisation, occupational pensions are of little value to workers who frequently change employer and costs of administering the scheme are thereby reduced. Equally understandably, seasonal workers are not entitled to paid time off during their temporary employment since they are employed to provide manpower at peak periods. In some cases they accrue entitlements to holiday pay which they receive as a lump sum on the termination of their employment, although in the holiday camps sector these accrued holiday entitlements are less than the holiday entitlements of comparable regular staff. In retailing and entertainment some organisations give no holiday pay at all.

Fixed-term versus open-ended contracts

It might also be thought that seasonal workers would be distinguished from their regular counterparts by special contracts of employment. However, this was far from always true. Some organisations do make use of fixed-term contracts, but by no means all do so. Some employ seasonal workers on indefinite contracts identical to those used for permanent workers.

Many retailing organisations said they gave fixed-term contracts to seasonal workers brought in to cope with the Christmas peak. Such contracts are appropriate because the timing and level of the peak can be determined with a high degree of certainty. Yet even in these circumstances some organisations use open-ended contracts and merely issue the statutory one week's notice of dismissal at the appropriate point in the season. Retailers hiring staff to meet summer peaks are less likely to use simple fixed-term contracts. Some give open-ended contracts, others employ their seasonal workers on a succession of fixed-term contracts of essentially an arbitrary duration (usually between 10 and 12 weeks) which contain an additional clause allowing the employer to terminate them prematurely with one weeks' notice. The reason for this is that the length of the season, and the level of activity within it, is less predictable than at Christmas time. It depends upon the weather and the number of visitors at the resorts, and greater flexibility is required than can be provided by simple fixed-term contracts.

Similar arguments for the need for flexibility were given by employers in the entertainments industry who recruit their seasonal staff on open-ended contracts and, more particularly, by employers in the holiday camps sector. Such contracts enable the latter to adjust their

115

seasonal labour force downwards to cope with any less busy periods within the summer season and, more important, to run their labour forces down gradually as the season draws to an end and the number of guests tails off.

Organisations using open-ended contracts always make clear in the course of recruiting staff and making formal job offers that the employment is seasonal. Moreover, although employers in the holiday camps sector themselves reserve the right to terminate seasonal workers' employment before the end of the season when the site finally shuts down, they seldom have to exercise this right. Students tend to leave towards the end of the season in order to take a vacation before returning to college; but it is not only amongst this group that turnover levels are high. Most camps employ two or more times as many people in the course of the summer than they would actually be recorded as employing on any one day, even in the height of the season. This allows for all but the most exceptional fluctuations in guest numbers to be managed with ease. Those wanting to stay throughout the season do so, but they constitute only about a quarter of initial recruitments and come disproportionately from the category of 'persons who work in the holiday industry' and usually occupy the more skilled jobs. In the entertainments industry, too, it was suggested that seasonal staff exhibited much higher rates of turnover than regular staff. This often made formal terminations at the end of the season unnecessary.

Our description of short-term contract working in one of its most traditional forms - seasonal working - has shown that temporary workers cannot always be distinguished from regular workers simply by reference to the contract of employment under which they work. It also suggests that there can be substantial differences between temporary workers and regular workers in terms of their characteristics and attachment to the labour force. How far these findings apply to short-term contract working in the manufacturing sector is the subject of the following section.

The 'new' short-term contract working in manufacturing

In some respects, temporary working in manufacturing is as traditional as it is in those parts of the service sector we have just examined.

However, in recent years much attention has been given to how manufacturing organisations have been negotiating or imposing its introduction or substantial extension. How widespread this development has been is difficult to judge. The fact that the specialist literature (for example, IRS, 1986a) continues to make repeated reference to the particular practices of a rather limited number of organisations implies that it is not, as yet, a particularly common one. Nevertheless, certain commentators (particularly Atkinson, 1984; Meager, 1985) have seized upon these or similar examples and presented them as showing the direction which personnel policy (and here their writings are rather unclear) is, or should be taking to cope with the challenges posed by a rapidly changing, increasingly competitive economic environment.

In the following paragraphs we look in more detail at the reasons which have encouraged a number of large manufacturers to start making or make greater use of temporary workers, at the terms and conditions under which these temporary workers are engaged, especially the forms of contract which are used, and at the characteristics of the temporary workers themselves.

'Economic uncertainty' and the search for 'flexibility'

The organisations we studied were involved in a widely differing range of activities. They included food manufacturers and processors, electronics and electrical goods manufacturers and companies engaged in various types of engineering work and metal production. They did, however, have certain features in common. Some food producers mentioned an increasing unpredictability in consumer tastes, some engineering companies a growing volatility in demand for their products. A number of organisations from both sectors spoke of the problems of an increase in the number of firms competing to supply particular markets, whilst a number were introducing new products onto the market and were unsure how these would fare. Some engineering companies had experienced a decline in demand for their traditional output and were moving into new areas which, if more buoyant, did not offer the same continuity as those in which they had previously operated. One of the electronics companies was staying in a declining market and trying to increase its share by increasing its competitiveness.

One engineering company was simultaneously undertaking a major retraining exercise for its staff to increase their effectiveness. The food manufacturers and processors and certain of the electrical goods producers also experienced seasonal fluctuations in their business activities.

In an attempt to keep labour costs to a minimum none of the organisations wanted to employ any more labour than was absolutely necessary. At the same time they wanted to be able to increase their staffing as and when orders came along, and did not want to be in a position to have to refuse orders because they did not have the staff, or lose them because they could not promise fast enough delivery. Equally, they wanted to be able to reduce their manpower as orders were completed and did not want to have to carry excess staff during slack periods. Several mentioned that in recent years the rate of voluntary leaving had decreased so that they were no longer able to rely upon increasing or slowing down the rate of recruitment to maintain their labour forces at the desired level.

A number of engineering firms had redundancy pay schemes granting compensation considerably in excess of that required by law and available to all those dismissed for economic reasons regardless of their length of service. Because of the financial costs of declaring redundancies, these firms were reluctant to add to their regular workforces. Several firms, in both food processing and engineering, felt that productivity and competitiveness could be enhanced if they could guarantee security of employment to what they regarded as their 'core' staff. However, they recognised that if they were to do this, they would also be required to create a 'buffer stock' of less protected workers to ensure that operational flexibility was maintained.

In general the jobs for which temporary workers were used were relatively low skilled. Some required a brief period - at most several days - of off-the-job training. After that, even though the workers might not be able to achieve maximum output, they were able to participate in production. However, we did find some manufacturing organisations, all in enginering, employing temporary workers in highly skilled positions. To some extent they were able to rely upon the generality of an engineering craftsman's training. More importantly they were also recruiting persons whom they had been obliged to make redundant in the face of earlier downturns and who were fully conversant with their own particular operations. Had such appropriately skilled ex-employees not been available in the local labour market, these organisations could not have entertained their strategies of using temporary workers in the first place.

We did encounter one organisation, again in engineering, which appeared to invest quite heavily in the training of persons it was recruiting on a temporary basis. Whilst the jobs in question were production line rather than craft jobs, the off-the-job training necessary to produce competent operators lasted (with interruptions) at least three weeks. In this case the duration of time spent in training constituted a not insubstantial part of the total duration of the contracts upon which most of the temporary workers were initially recruited (six months). The organisation's behaviour would appear to be explained by an expectation that the increased demand for output which had led it to bring in temporary workers would, in fact, be sustained. This optimism seemed justified, since after our visit all temporary workers were upgraded to permanent status.

The limits imposed by trade unions

In all the manufacturing organisations we studied, trade unions had been involved in plans to introduce or extend temporary working. In some cases, particularly the non-engineering companies, the extent to which they had been able to shape these plans as opposed merely to sanction them was very limited indeed. Even in the engineering companies the role of the unions seemed to have been limited to ensuring that, in other than their temporary status, temporary workers were not disadvantaged and received the same fringe benefits (except membership of company pension schemes) as regular workers. In the food manufacturing and processing and electronics and electrical goods companies, where unions were relatively weaker, there were more likely to be differences between regular and temporary workers in this last respect. However, some of these could be explained by the fact that the temporary workers were also part-timers (who were, in any case, excluded from particular benefits), or that certain benefits were available only to workers with a minimum service record.

In two of the engineering companies the unions had insisted that temporary workers be guaranteed a minimum period of employment. The duration of this period was determined by what was understood to be the minimum length of time that an unemployed person would have to work in order to re-open rights to unemployment benefits. In one case, however, a misunderstanding of what are admittedly very unclear social security regulations meant that the minimum period was twice as long as would have been necessary to satisfy this objective. In some engineering and food manufacturing and processing companies unions had also imposed a maximum duration to all temporary employment, and all temporary workers achieving such service had to be given permanent status. These maximum durations varied widely, from as little as nine months to as long as two years.

In some instances unions had set a limit on the size of the temporary labour force expressed as a proportion of the total or the regular labour force, and if this limit was exceeded an equivalent number of temporary workers would have to be upgraded to permanent status. Subject to some negotiation, the level of any such limits was set by reference to what the organisation considered to be its 'core' level of business, and again there were substantial variations to be observed. We encountered limits as low as 10 per cent and as high as 30 per cent. In other cases there were no restrictions on numbers of temporary workers or the duration of their employment, merely a requirement to inform or consult about their use. One company had obtained a concession from its local unions to employ *at least* a certain proportion of its workforce on a temporary basis.

Until not long ago several of the national unions whose local officers or shop stewards had negotiated the kind of agreements just described were fiercely opposed to the introduction or use of temporary workers. As we have already seen, this is now changing. The Confederation of Shipbuilding and Engineering Unions took temporary workers on board insofar as it took steps to develop a coherent policy on their use for recommendation to affiliated unions (see IRS, 1986b). The clerical workers union (APEX) did the same (see IRS, 1987). The Transport and General Workers Union and the General and Municipal Union have gone further. The former has drawn up a model agreement for its local officials which specify the conditions under which temporary workers may and may not be used, and require that they be treated in all other respects as regular members of the enterprise's labour force. The latter has put together very similar 'guidelines' for use by its negotiators on the ground (ibid).

Even more radical steps have been taken by the electricians union (EETPU). Local officials in Essex have reached agreements with three enterprises in the town of Harlow which not only regulate the use of temporary workers but also establish a list of its (otherwise unemployed) members who are available for temporary jobs. When the enterprises concerned need temporary workers, they will recruit from this list (see IRS 1986c). Such registers have long been maintained by unions in industries where there is a tradition of using temporary workers - for example by the printers union (NGA) for the supply of casual labour to newspaper printing companies, and by the draughtsmens union (TASS) for the supply of 'casual' or temporary drawing office staff. The EETPU Essex agreements are the first instance of this practice being extended into the field of the 'new' temporary working.

The choice of contractual form

Just as the temporary status of the seasonal labour in the service sector was by no means always obvious by reference only to their contracts of employment, neither was that of the 'new' temporary labour force in manufacturing. Several of the engineering companies visited did recruit their temporary workers on simple fixed-term contracts. Sometimes this was with good reason. Their manpower requirements were planned in detail and they knew exactly when and for how long they needed additional workers. Sometimes this form of contract appeared less appropriate. The organisations faced uncertainty and it was not clear whether the time when they might need to reduce their labour force would coincide with the date of expiry of a fixed-term contract. One organisation had responded to such a situation by issuing fixed-term contracts for a period equivalent to its minimum planned needs and then retaining the workers concerned on one week's notice, with no obligation to negotiate their dismissal with the trade unions if their services were still required thereafter.

121

Most of the organisations in food processing and manufacturing and in electronics and electrical goods employed their temporary workers on open-ended contracts. Some of them had previously experimented with fixed-term contracts but had found they imposed too much rigidity. Either they had been obliged to renew such contracts, perhaps several times, and had thus come under pressure to give the workers concerned permanent status, or they had found themselves carrying workers whose fixed-term contracts had not yet expired, despite the fact that they were no longer needed. However, the open-ended contracts they had introduced instead made clear that the workers concerned were employed on a different basis from other members of the labour force. For example, the dismissal of temporary workers did not require the same consultations or negotiations to be opened with the trade unions as would be necessary if redundancies amongst the regular labour force were proposed. The unions concerned had, in effect, given an advance commitment not to contest the redundancies of the temporary workers.[3] Moreover, the notice that had to be given to temporary workers was always the statutory minimum (one week if, as was usual, they had less than two years service) rather than the extended notice (often a minimum of four weeks) which many of the organisations had granted to their regular workforces. Equally, enhanced redundancy compensation schemes, such as had been negotiated for the regular workers at several of the organisations to which we spoke, did not apply to the temporary workers, who (unless they have at least two years' service) were also ineligible for any statutory payments. Two organisations which we visited further emphasised the 'non-regularity' of their temporary workers' employment by not guaranteeing them any fixed number of hours work per week - they were contracted to work 'as and when required' - and this, of course, provided them with an important, additional source of flexibility. One of them had also set a maximum on the number of hours that would be offered, so that whilst its regular labour force was largely full-time, its temporary labour force worked no more than three-quarter time.

The 'new' temporary workers

Short-term contract working in manufacturing differed from short-term contract or seasonal working in the three service sectors described above and, indeed, from the other forms of temporary working we have examined in this study, in that many of the temporary workers concerned were 'involuntary' temporary workers. Each of the organisations with which we had contact was a major or even the dominant local employer, and each was located in an area of high unemployment. Most of those recruited into temporary positions were seeking permanent employment, even if, particularly in the food manufacturing and processing companies, they were often seeking part-time rather than full-time permanent jobs. Nevertheless, it is by no means certain that the 'new' temporary workers are very different from more traditional temporary workers in manufacturing in this respect. Using LFS data, Table 7.1 shows that temporary workers in semi- and lower skilled industrial occupations are more likely to be working on this basis because they have been unable to find permanent jobs than temporary workers in general and particularly than temporary workers in lower level service occupations, who are more likely to be working on this basis because they do not want permanent jobs. Table 7.1 thus also supports the contention made in the first half of this chapter that short-term contract workers in the service sector are mainly 'voluntary' temporary workers.

Although all of the organisations studied were recruiting only into temporary jobs, in some organisations temporary jobs offered a step on the way to regular employment. This was obviously so in organisations which were expanding and which, as a consequence, either found themselves exceeding the agreed limits on the size of their temporary labour forces or felt confident of being able to make commitments to a greater number of workers. Some of the organisations studied had upgraded the status of large numbers of their temporary workers for this reason in the past, some were in the process of doing so. Where no expansion was taking place, the only chance of transfer was if vacancies arose in the regular workforce. Promotion was then usually based upon seniority, sometimes upon performance. One organisation, which faced a marked seasonal demand for its output and made substantial hirings once a year, reserved its temporary vacancies for school leavers. As the season drew to a close it actively encouraged early retirement and voluntary redundancy amongst its older or less productive workers and filled the resulting vacancies with the most productive temporary workers. Explicit use of temporary working as a means of facilitating selection was, however, rare.

Some of the organisations which had been utilising temporary workers for a number of years had people in their temporary workforce who had been employed by them several times, sometimes for several months at a time, and who had not worked elsewhere in the interim. Courts, if they had been called upon to investigate these people's employment protection rights, might well have deemed someof them to have had one continuous employment relationship broken only by shortages of work rather than a series of different relationships[4]. Some of the employers were beginning to recognise this. We found a few examples of workers who had been in the uninterrupted employment of a single organisation long enough to qualify for dismissal protection and statutory redundancy compensation rights, but who still had temporary status. Most managers disapproved of such a state of affairs and suggested that they would not permit it, but where unions were weak and the competitive pressures upon employers intense, its evidence is understandable.

Is temporary working a threat to regular working?

Examples such as this last raise the issue of the extent to which employers in manufacturing are using temporary working as a substitute for the recruitment of employees on a regular basis. In a trivial sense, of course, they are. It is, however, important to consider what the organisations might have done had they not resorted to this form of flexibility. Few could have met their demands for additional labour internally, and not because they were hampered by rigid job demarcation systems or lacked a workforce with adaptable skills. Some could have increased overtime working, but for those using continuous or semi-continuous production processes this was technically difficult, and for those employing mainly women largely infeasible. Others considered bringing in temporary workers only when the practical limits of overtime working had been reached. Most temporary workers were fired as well as hired, and the implication is that if they had not been used the organisations concerned would have had to practise some other form of 'hire and fire' strategy. Given the importance of the 'last in, first out' principle in British industry, the experiences of many members of the temporary labour force would have been little different from what they actually were. Calling them 'temporary workers' merely made their situation clear to them from the start of their employment.

It should also be borne in mind that the employment security of the regular labour force depends upon the employment insecurity of the temporary labour force. This proposition can be considered at two levels. First, many of the agreements governing the introduction or extension of the use of temporary workers simultaneously contained job guarantees for the regular labour force. These protected members from temporary lay-offs - of some importance in certain organisations in food manufacturing and electrical goods which experienced seasonal or predicable fluctuations in demand for output - and from compulsory redundancies, and they were welcomed. The trade union officials involved in the agreements were fully aware of their two-sided nature, and some admitted to a sense of bad conscience at seeing the regular dismissal of 'involuntary' temporary workers. Many, however, also pointed out that the organisations in which they were working had little alternative to some recourse to temporary working. Their view was that at least they had secured the best possible conditions for the temporary workers (equal pay and, as far as possible, fringe benefits) and/or had made sure that their use was kept to a minimum and was subject to continuous monitoring.

Second, if it is accepted that the organisations in question were operating in highly competitive markets, then their ability to win orders did necessitate an ability to adjust their manpower levels upwards and downwards and to hold labour costs to a minimum. Their use of temporary workers provided a means of meeting these needs. Had they not had such a resource at their disposal some might have had to forego particular orders, others might have been obliged to withdraw entirely from certain markets, whilst still others would have been less willing to innovate with new products offering chances of survival or expansion. In each case the implications for their regular labour forces would have been negative. There might be other solutions open to organisations facing similar pressures (one, 'cooperative production', is somewhat idealistically proposed by Piore, 1986), but using temporary workers was probably the easiest to put into effect.

To finish, we should emphasise that the kind of short-term contract working we have observed in manufacturing is a specific phenomenon. In periods when demand for output is high, it is unlikely to be found. Organisations can afford to miss orders or propose later deliveries and are not obliged to exercise such rigid control upon their labour costs. Nor, in tight labour markets, would they find the workers willing to accept employment on a temporary basis. Despite the security which full employment offers them, most workers would wish to be able to decide for themselves when to terminate any particular employment. Full employment, competition between employers for labour and high levels of labour turnover might mean that many people are working for only a short time in any particular job. Some might choose to describe these persons as 'temporary workers', but if they did they would have to recognise that they are also 'voluntary' temporary workers.

Conclusions
In terms of the numbers of persons involved, short-term contract working (with the worker being the direct employee of the organisation which engages him) is the most important form of temporary working in Britain. Much of it is concentrated in sectors which face a seasonal demand for their output or services and its practice is long established. In the past few years there have been signs of its introduction and extension by manufacturing organisations experiencing increasing volatility in their markets, increasing inability to predict their manpower requirements and increasing pressures to minimise labour costs.

The practices of organisations in all of the sectors studied suggest that fixed-term contracts are by no means the only way in which short-term contract workers can be recruited. Indeed, for all but those organisations which know precisely how much additional manpower they need and for how long, in their simple form they are a particularly unsuitable means of employing temporary workers. They are appropriate for some of the very regular peaks which occur in the retailing sector, but are highly inappropriate for the uncertainty with which many manufacturing organisations are having to cope. Many short-term contract workers are, as a consequence, employed on open-ended contracts and distinguished from regular employees by other terms and conditions of their employment and, where relevant, by the agreement of trade unions not to contest their dismissal. Particularly in the manufacturing sector we have found organisations searching for the most satisfactory form of distinguishing temporary from regular staff.

There appear to be substantial differences between the 'traditional' temporary workers employed in seasonal jobs in such sectors as retailing, entertainments and the holiday industry and the 'new' temporary workers employed in some organisations in the manufacturing sector. The proportion of the former who are not interested in regular working, because they have other interests or other commitments, is relatively high, although it is influenced by the level of unemployment overall as well as in the local labour market. On the other hand, many of the latter are 'involuntary' temporary workers. In the manufacturing sector, an employer's ability to pursue a strategy of using temporary workers depends on the availability of a body of labour which, until a few years ago, scarcely existed.

Where trade unions have been involved at the level of the enterprise they have generally not sought to resist the introduction of temporary workers. Rather they have tried to regulate the conditions under which such workers are employed. They have recognised the necessity of temporary working given the particular circumstances of the enterprise concerned, and have sought, where possible, to ensure that temporary workers otherwise enjoy the same terms and conditions as regular workers. They have also found themselves agreeing to the introduction of temporary workers in return for employers granting increased job security for the majority of the labour force. The stance of the (same) unions nationally has, until recently, been rather different. Outside those sectors where temporary working has a long tradition, they have usually vigorously condemned it. Their position has, however, started to change - sometimes quite radically. They too have come to accept temporary working and, by showing concern for their conditions of employment, are making temporary workers one of the main targets of their recruitment drives.

Short-term contract working in its traditional form has not been a subject of substantial political or academic concern, but questions have been asked as to whether the 'new' short-term contract working in manufacturing is displacing regular working or undermining the conditions of the regular labour force. We suggest that, whilst there might appear to be a substitution of temporary for regular workers, the alternative to temporary working would probably be more hiring and firing and more temporary lay-offs. The 'new' short-term contract working is a conjuncturally specific phenomenon which will recede in importance as the pressures which have induced its appearance weaken.

Notes

1. Indeed, in this latter case a casual and a short-term contract worker are in many ways indistinguishable, since, as we have seen in Chapter 1, it is only after four weeks employment that a worker is entitled to a minimum period of notice.

2. Because of their irregular participation in the labour market most seasonal workers would not have paid or had credited to them sufficient social security contributions to be eligible for the alternative, less generous state sickness benefit.

3. he statutory obligations to consult trade unions over redundancies contained in employment protection law (see IDS, 1982) remain in force, but they are reduced to a formality.

4. One personnel manager who was experiencing such a situation made reference to the recent 'Flack v. Kodak case' (see IR5, 1985b). In this case, workers who had been employed on a intermittent basis for a number of years were found to have been continuously employed (albeit with temporary cessations due to shortages of work) and thus, when finally dismissed, entitled to full redundancy compensation.

Table 7.1   Reasons for taking temporary employment given by lower level workers with industrial and service occupations

Percentages

	Job includes training	Could not find perm. job	Did not find perm. job	Other/ no reason	(n) 000s
all temporary workers	5.2	35.6	27.1	32.1	(1,493)
lower level service and supervisory jobs	2.6	29.7	38.4	29.3	(560)

Source: 1984 LFS

8 Temporary employment in Britain: summary

An analysis of the extent and nature of temporary employment relationships in Britain requires an acceptable definition of the term 'temporary'. This is not straightforward. It is not easy to say what the 'permanent' employment relationship is with which the 'temporary' one is to be contrasted? Unlike in certain other European countries, British labour law sets no maximum duration to a temporary employment relationship, whereby all persons employed for longer than a certain period of time automatically have permanent status. British labour law merely gives employees rights dependent upon their length of service. Providing they have attained the relevant service, all employees - regardless of the 'temporariness' or 'permanence' of their employment - are treated the same [see Chapter 1].

If we cannot specify temporary workers in general, at least we can do so in particular. From the literature we were able to identify 11 categories of worker referred to as temporary workers. These were:

(1) consultants and freelancers; (2) labour only sub-contractors; (3) casual workers; (4) seasonal workers; (5) fixed-term contract workers; (6) workers with a contract dischargeable by performance; (7) workers on training contracts; (8) temporary workers on indefinite contracts; (9) agency workers; (10) employees of works contractors; (11) participants in special programmes for the unemployed [see Overview 1 of Chapter 1].

Many of these categories overlap each other. Thus labour only sub-contractors can be viewed as a sub-category of free lancers and certain workers on training contracts as a sub-category of workers on performance contracts. Equally, seasonal workers might be engaged on a casual basis, on fixed-term or performance contracts, or even on open-ended contracts. Participants in job creation programmes are usually employed on fixed-term contracts, whilst those in special training schemes might be considered as workers on a training contract. Some consultants and freelancers market their services via an agency, and some employees of works contractors closely resemble agency workers. In addition, the terms used have different meanings in different circumstances. A good example of this is the way in which 'casual' is used as a pejorative for 'temporaries' (for example, the 1986 conference of the engineering workers union, AUEW, passed a motion which 'attacked the greater use of casual workers by employers').

The size of the temporary labour force

The multiplicity of terms used to describe temporary workers, and the way in which they overlap, makes measurement of the size of the temporary labour force difficult. Since there is no single, objective definition of 'temporary', measurement attempts which have been made have had to rely upon subjective definitions, either of workers or of employers. A worker-directed study conducted in the mid-1970s considered as temporary workers all who had a job which was available only for a limited time and all who were themselves available for their jobs for only a limited period of time. On this basis, some 7 per cent of the labour force could be classified as 'temporary'. Nevertheless, it seems that only just over half of all temporary workers were in jobs which themselves were not temporary. An inquiry directed at a not necessarily random sample of employers in 1984 asked about the number of workers they had whose stay with the organisation was recognised by both sides as being temporary. Grossing up their results the authors of the inquiry suggested that just over 7 per cent of all jobs in the economy were temporary. We suspect that temporary worker users were more likely to respond to such a survey and that its findings might be an over-estimate [see Chapter 1].

131

Our own efforts to examine the overall size of the temporary workforce were centred upon a special analysis of the British/European Communities Labour Force Survey (LFS). This survey asks workers to categorise their job as 'permanent' or 'temporary', but again there is nothing to stop those who regard their own availability for a job as short-term from categorising themselves as temporary workers. According to the 1984 LFS rather over 6 per cent of the labour force considered themselves to be working on a temporary basis.

As might be expected the temporary workforce was disproportionately concentrated in the service sector, in particular in the distribution, hotels and catering industries and in 'other' services, both public and private (in Britain this includes public administration). These two broad industrial groups account for rather less than half the total labour force but nearly two-thirds of the temporary labour force [see Table 2.1]. Reflecting this is the way in which temporary workers are found in service sector occupations. Again it was no surprise to find most temporary workers in what could best be described as lower level or less skilled occupations, both in industry and services [see Table 2.2]. However, the LFS also showed a higher than average level of temporary working amongst certain highly skilled workers, most notably teachers and nurses. In these cases the skills concerned are general rather than specific to one employer, precisely as human capital theory would suggest.

Forms of temporary working

The British LFS permits temporary workers to differentiate themselves between those engaged on a seasonal, temporary or casual basis and those contracted to work for a fixed period of time or to undertake a fixed task. These two forms of temporary working are by no means mutually exclusive, and to classify oneself as in the second group requires more detailed knowledge of contractual status. Nevertheless, some patterns did emerge. About two-thirds of all temporary workers put themselves into the seasonal, temporary or casual category, though the proportion was much higher amongst those in lower level occupations and much lower amongst those in more skilled, and particularly in 'professional' occupations [see Table 2.4]. Equally, temporary workers in manufacturing industry, regardless of occupation, were more likely to be employed on fixed-term contracts or for fixed tasks. The LFS also allows agency workers to be distinguished, but these make up only some 50,000 of the 1.5m temporary workers in Britain. Most of them are to be found in a narrow range of occupations and over half are office or secretarial workers [see Table 2.5]. The explanation is not that the occupations concerned contain a substantially higher than average share of temporary workers, but rather that a higher than average proportion of the temporary workers concerned supply their services via an agency. Nearly three-quarters of all agency workers live in the South East of England, the only significant regional disparity with respect to the incidence of temporary working we discovered.

One finding of our LFS analysis was that temporary workers often overlapped with other forms of 'non-standard' worker - namely self-employed and part-time workers [see Diagram 1 in Chapter 2]. A rather higher proportion of temporary workers are self-employed than are all workers (15 per cent compared to 11 per cent). A considerable number come from industries where the overall rate of self-employment is above average, such as construction, or have occupations best described as 'professional', but they also include many low-skilled industrial and service sector workers. More dramatic is the overlap between part-time and temporary workers. Whilst only just over a fifth of all workers work on a part-time basis, well over a half of temporary workers do so. In industries such as retail distribution, catering and personal services, where a high proportion of the total labour force is, in any case, part-time, over 80 per cent of temporary workers are part-timers. Conversely, most of the more highly skilled temporary workers work full-time [see Table 2.7]. The one exception to this is teachers, and this might result from the fact that many education authorities (teachers' employers) give all part-time teachers temporary contracts. The incidence of part-time working is much higher amongst those with seasonal, temporary or casual jobs than those with fixed term contract jobs (69 per cent as opposed to 25 per cent). This suggests that 'seasonal' and more particularly 'casual' workers and part-time workers are functional equivalents.

A higher proportion of the temporary than the total labour force are women (54 per cent compared to 41 per cent). This is largely to be explained by the industrial and occupational distribution of temporary jobs and the overlap between temporary working and part-time working. Female temporary workers are more likely to have low skilled, part-time, seasonal, temporary or casual jobs, whilst male temporary workers are more likely to have more skilled, full-time, fixed-term contract jobs. Temporary workers are also considerably younger than the generality of workers, largely because a high proportion of them are still teenagers. Indeed, nearly one in five of all temporary workers are under 20 and a quarter of all teenagers in the labour force work on a temporary basis. In all other age groups below retirement age the proportion of temporary workers is lower than the average for all age groups. Some explanation for the high concentration of young persons in the temporary workforce are discussed in the following paragraphs where we look at reasons for taking temporary jobs.

Reasons for taking temporary jobs

The single most important reason for taking a temporary job given by respondents to the LFS was that a permanent job was not available [see Table 2.10]. However, this reason was offered by little more than a third of all temporary workers. Rather more than a quarter did not want a permanent job. There were substantial differences between men and women, with four in ten of the former giving this as their principal reason and only 16 per cent claiming they did not want a permanent job. For women, on the other hand, not wanting a permanent job was the single most important reason given (37 per cent). Fewer would have preferred a permanent job (29 per cent). For married women the tendency was even more pronounced, as it also was for part-time temporary workers (43 per cent did not want a permanent job against 8 per cent of full- timers) and for those with seasonal, temporary or casual as opposed to fixed-term contract jobs (36 per cent against 10 per cent). In each of these cases, the proportion of temporary workers who could be described as 'voluntary' temporary workers (i.e. not wanting a permanent job) was much higher than the proportion who could be described as 'involuntary' (i.e. unable to get a permanent job). Lastly, although there was no great regional disparity in the incidence of temporary working, there were marked differences between regions in the proportion of temporary workers who could be described as 'involuntary' temporary workers. There was a clear and direct relationship between the level of unemployment in the region and the proportion of temporary workers working on this basis 'involuntarily' [see Table 4.1].

Only a small minority (5 per cent) of all temporary workers had taken such jobs because they were tied to a course of training, and most of these were young adults. However, nearly a third of teenagers with temporary jobs were still at school [see Table 2.12]. The jobs they held were either evening/weekend ones (and so part-time) or vacation ones. Whether or not these jobs were available only for a short period of time, they were regarded by their holders as temporary. Of course, those temporary workers still at school did not want permanent jobs. In the same way, a large proportion of temporary workers over pension age had taken their temporary jobs 'voluntarily' rather than 'involuntarily'. Another very important reason why many teenagers were temporary workers is that they were simultaneously participants in special government employment measures. A third of all teenage temporary workers fell into this category, and most of them were in training positions under the Youth Training Scheme. In all, more than one in eight of all temporary workers were participants in special measures, with a job creation scheme - the Community Programme - accounting for most of those aged 20 or above.

Temporary work as a way into and out of employment

Insofar as it provides information on their situation one year ago, the LFS enables us to see how many persons enter employment via temporary jobs. Approximately a quarter of those unemployed 12 months ago but in work on the survey date were employed on a temporary basis, compared to just over three per cent of those in employment at both dates. Equally, just over a third of those who had been out of the labour market altogether, but were now in work, had temporary jobs. We expect that a considerable number of these were teenagers with occasional/part- time jobs or school leavers picked up by special employment measures. Of 'voluntary' temporary workers, nearly a half had been out of the labour market entirely 12 months before and only two per cent had been unemployed, but of 'involuntary' temporary workers the proportions were just under one third in both cases.

The importance of temporary jobs as a stepping stone out of unemployment is supported by the Unemployed Flow Survey undertaken by PSI in conjunction with the Manpower Services Commission. A special analysis of this showed that a quarter of all people entering unemployment in May 1980 who had found a job within 10 months had taken one which they knew to be temporary. A rather higher proportion (35 per cent) treated their job as a 'stop-gap' and were looking for other work [see Table 4.2].

An importanat question is whether the coming to an end of a temporary job is a major contributor to flows into unemployment. Here the Unemployed Flow Survey and the LFS gave somewhat different results. According to the first, only a very small proportion (6 per cent) of those entering unemployment from employment did so because a temporary job had come to an end; according to the second rather more (16 per cent) did. Both surveys, however, suggested that redundancy, dismissals and even voluntary leaving were much more important reasons for entry into unemployment.

Using the Unemployed Flow Survey data we were also able to see whether there was any relationship between temporary jobs and recurrent unemployment. Those people whose first job on leaving unemployment was a 'temporary' one were more likely to suffer multiple spells of unemployment, to hold many jobs, to experience a longer time in unemployment and a shorter time in employment over the 20 months following their initial registration than those whose first job was a 'permanent' one [see Tables 4.3-5]. An even clearer result was that, of those who had entered into unemployment because a temporary job had come to an end and who found a new job within 10 months, nearly twice as many (44 per cent) took temporary jobs as did the generality of those finding work (25 per cent) [see Table 4.6]. This suggests that, for at least some people, labour market activity is characterised by a pattern of working in short-term jobs punctuated by spells of unemployment. We do not, however, know whether this reflects voluntary behaviour, whether it is a result of deficiencies of the individuals concerned, or of the situation in the local/occupational labour market in which they are located.

Employers' use of temporary workers
The only representative study containing information on employers' use of temporary workers is the Workplace Industrial Relations Survey (WIRS) conducted by the Department of Employment together with PSI. It covered some 2,000 establishments in all sectors of the economy. Although WIRS concentrated on issues such as collective bargaining, wage determination and grievance resolution, it did ask whether the establishment concerned made use of staff employed on fixed-term contracts and agency workers. In 1984, 20 per cent of all establishments were using at least one fixed-term contract worker, and a third of these (seven per cent) were using a number equivalent to at least five per cent of their labour force. About 17 per cent were using at least one agency worker and, again, a third of these (six per cent) were using a number equivalent to at least five per cent of their labour force. The practices of private manufacturing and private service sector establishments were very similar. Just over a tenth (11-12 per cent) of each used fixed-term contract workers and just over a fifth (22 per cent) of each used agency workers. Establishments in public administration (particularly in education) made the greatest use of fixed-term contract workers - 39 per cent did so - and the least use of agency workers - eight per cent did so [see Tables 3.1-2].

WIRS could also be used to examine some of the characteristics of private sector establishments using fixed-term contract and agency workers. When the number of fixed-term contract or agency workers was expressed in relation to the size of the total labour force in the establishment, it did not appear that larger establishments were more likely to make use of temporary workers than smaller ones [see Table 3.4]. Some commentators had predicted otherwise, suggesting that larger organisations, pursuing more sophisticated personnel policies, would be more ready to exploit the advantages offered by such employment forms. In line with what we had expected was the finding that establishments where the level of output, the amount of overtime being worked and the number of persons employed was falling were rather less likely to be using fixed-term contract workers. On the other hand, there was no clear relationship between economic performance and the use of agency workers, suggesting that the two types of temporary workers are not close equivalents [see Tables 3.5-8].

Contrary to what is implied in much of the recent discussion of the 'flexible firm' we found that establishments using either of the two forms of temporary worker were, in general, no more (or less) likely than other establishments to use certain other forms of 'non-standard' worker - namely part-timers, freelancers and homeworkers - which the survey identified [see Tables 3.14-15]. There were some indications that users of freelancers might make slightly greater use of agency workers, but equally that high users of part-timers tended to be lower users of agency workers. In addition, although users of fixed-term contract workers were more likely to use agency workers (and vice versa), the differences were small.

Reasons for using temporary workers

Our analysis of the available statistical sources on employers' use of the extent of temporary working was complemented by interviews with personnel managers and, as appropriate, trade union representatives from industries, enterprises and establishments where various types of temporary worker were to be found. We wanted to learn more about the reasons why they employed labour on this basis and about the terms under which the engagement was made. We also inquired further about the extent to which temporary workers received training from their employers. We concentrated on retailing, the leisure/holidays and the catering industries, on manufacturing enterprises and on organisations supplying agency workers.

In retailing and the leisure/holidays industries, seasonal fluctuations in demand provided the principal explanation for the resort to temporary workers [see Chapter 7]. However, in some sectors of manufacturing too - particularly food processing, but also such sectors as consumer electrical goods - strong seasonal patterns of demand were experienced. In retailing, 'seasons' were fairly short, the most important covering the month or two before Christmas and the 'sales' period immediately afterwards; in the holidays industry they could be very much longer, covering the entire period from late Spring to early Autumn. Moreover, whilst in the retailing sector enterprises might supplement their labour forces by about 10 per cent to cope with seasonal peaks, in the holidays sector the increase made might be as high as several hundred per cent. Almost the entire labour force might be made up of seasonal workers. The catering industry as a whole experiences seasonal demands for additional labour but, more important, those firms which provide catering for special 'events' - exhibitions, cultural sporting or social occasions - have to cope with dramatic day-to-day variations in their demand for labour [see Chapter 6]. For the few hours, the day or few days' duration of the 'event', their labour force at the location in question increases many times in size. Casual workers are what they use, and the short duration of each 'event' is an important explanation of the overlap between part-time and casual working.

Demand for temporary workers of these kinds has often been labelled 'traditional' in its nature. In contrast to this is the 'new' demand for temporary workers said to be experienced, or likely to be experienced on an increasing scale, by enterprises in the manufacturing sector. In the face of an economic climate characterised by a higher degree of 'uncertainty', a greater volatility in demand for their output and increased pressure to reduce labour costs to a minimum, employers are seeking to build in to their workforces an element of 'numerical flexibility'. This consists of workers who can be brought in and discharged as and when required or, more usually, without the need to enter into negotiations with trade unions, without being given more than the statutory minimum notice of dismissal, or without being paid more than the statutory minimum redundancy compensation [see Chapter 7].

Performing a function as interesting as that of the 'new' temporary workers in manufacturing are agency workers. The evidence of both the LFS and of the field work points to their flourishing in tight occupational and local labour markets [see Chapter 5]. Employers trying to secure particular categories of staff are often unable to adjust their own, bureaucratically determined, salary scales upwards without disrupting established diffentials or provoking claims for similar rises from their other employees. Pay rates for agency workers are determined in a 'spot market' and the existence of this spot market allows the local occupational labour market to clear. We observed this clearly in the Greater London and South-East England labour market for secretarial staff and in the South East England labour market for computer programmers and analysts. Employers were sometimes being obliged to fill what they considered 'permanent' positions with 'temporary' workers.

The nature of the employment relationship

Agency working has aroused interest in Britain not only because it is concentrated in particular local and occupational labour markets but also because of the special status that agency workers have in employment law. For tax and social security purposes most are treated as dependent employees, although a small number - mainly 'professionals' such as accountants or computer programmers - formally register themselves as self-employed. However, according to the decisions of labour courts, agency workers are not only not the employees of the client organisation or user firm, they are also not the employees of the agency which supplies them. Rather they are considered self-employed independent contractors.

Precisely the same appears to be the case for a numerically much more important group of temporary workers, casual workers. With respect to both agency workers and casual workers the courts have deemed that there is no obligation for the apparent employer (in the case of the agency worker, the agency) to offer work and no obligation on the worker to accept offers made. In the absence of such mutual obligation, it has been held, a relationship of employment does not exist. Accordingly, agency and casual workers are excluded from the rights accorded to most workers under employment protection legislation [see Chapters 5 and 6].

Such rulings have aroused concern amongst academic lawyers and other socio-legal researchers, but it has to be asked whether they are likely to have any far reaching impact. Our investigations of agency working indicated that the tight labour markets in which most agency workers operated gave them a high degree of de facto employment security, in the sense of a continuous stream of bookings, whatever their status in employment law [see Chapter 5]. Our investigations of casual working in the catering industry confirmed the impressions given by the data from the LFS that most casual workers did not want to work on a regular, continuous basis. Since most employment rights are dependent upon the possession of a record of continuous service with a single employer, most casual workers would fail to qualify for most of these rights even if they did have dependent employee status. Those who are working as agency or casual workers 'involuntarily', whilst looking for a more permanent job, are also, by definition, not interested in building up long-term relationships with their employers. Those few casual workers in the catering industry who do seem to work on a more or less continuous, almost full-time basis over a long period for a single organisation (the plaintiffs in the oft-cited 'O'Kelly case'), tend to possess skills which that organisation, and indeed other potential employers, value. Regardless of their peculiar labour law status, they too have a high degree of de facto employment security [see Chapter 6].

With respect to certain of the other temporary workers whose use we studied in more detail, it was not their employment status which was of interest but the way in which their 'temporariness' was distinguished [see Chapter 7]. As we suggested in the introduction, 'temporary' workers are normally thought of as those who are not engaged on indefinite contract of employment, and the obvious opposite of an indefinite contract of employment is a contract for a fixed period of time. Certainly, in many cases temporary workers are given fixed-term contracts, but that is not the only way in which they are engaged.

Where the requirement for additional labour can be specified precisely, and the organisation knows precisely how long it requires the staff concerned, fixed-term contracts are most appropriate. On the other hand, employers frequently do not know exactly how long they will need to make use of their temporary workers. They do not know how long a season will last (in the holidays industry the weather plays an important part), how long a permanent member of staff on long-term sick leave will be away, or how long an exceptional surge in demand will last. If they were to employ staff on fixed-term contracts, they could be creating rigidity for themselves rather than flexibility. They might find themselves having to issue a succession of fixed-term contracts to each worker, and having to take steps to include in these

141

contracts provisions for their premature termination. Instead, it is often simpler to make use of open-ended òr indefinite contracts, the same contracts as are applied to other, 'permanent' members of staff. We found temporary workers employed on òpen-ended contracts in the retailing industry, in the holidays industry and in manufacturing firms, particularly where temporary workers had been introduced as part of a strategy of managing 'uncertainty'.

If not all temporary workers are distinguishable by having been recruited for a pre-determined period of time, we might ask how they are distinguishable. They are always made aware of their temporary status on being recruited, but sometimes the only other difference between them and other members of the workforce is that the trade unions within the organisation have consented in advance not to contest the employer's right to dismiss them once he feels he no longer has any work for them. In the private service sector, where trade unions are less active, temporary workers often do not receive the same level of fringe benefits as permanent workers; and in some organisations and industries they are paid at a lower rate - for example the statutory minimum rather than a higher, collectively bargained rate - than are comparable permanent workers [see Chapter 7]. Casual workers in particular are paid only for hours worked and usually receive no fringe benefits at all [see Chapter 6]. Agency workers are also paid by the hour, but the larger agencies, competing for scarce labour, have increasingly started to offer fringe benefits such as sickness and holiday pay [see Chapter 5].

The training of temporary workers
Our investigations of temporary worker users revealed the same picture as economic theory would predict and as the LFS had indicated - that most temporary workers were occupying relatively low-skilled positions. The extent of formal training given by employing organisations was usually minimal, amounting to little more than an introduction, with other skills being learned on the job. Where temporary workers occupied skilled positions they were required to possess the relevant skills in advance. In most cases these skills were of a very general nature; in a few cases they were highly specific to the particular organisation. [see Chapter 7]. On these occasions those

temporary workers recruited were ex-employees - those who had been dismissed in recent downturns and who had been unable to find a new job.

Trade unions and temporary working

The data from WIRS did not always show that establishments where trade unions were recognised or where union density was high were also less likely than others to use temporary workers [see Table 3. 9-10], but there were good reasons to explain this - not least the absence of a question in the survey on employers' use of casual workers. WIRS did, however, suggest that large unionized manufacturing establishments were less likely to use agency workers [see Table 3.11]. Our explanation for this was that unions might feel they had less control over the conditions of indirectly employed temporary workers than over the conditions of those who are directly employed. If temporary workers are to be brought in, they will press for them to be of the latter category.

The general attitude of trade unions towards temporary working can best be described as hostile, the exception being in sectors such as retailing or holidays, where temporary working is traditional and largely accepted [see Chapter 7]. In hotels and catering, which also falls into the category of a 'traditional' temporary working sector, there has been union opposition to temporary working based on fears that casual workers were displacing regular staff [see Chapter 6]. Agency working, again a relatively 'traditional' form of temporary working, has also been vigorously rejected by unions, partly because of its association with the fee-charging private placement bureaux (which many agencies simultaneously are) to which they object as undermining the public employment service [see Chapter 5].

As they became conscious of the 'new' temporary working, the unions' initial response was to harden their historical stance. Union conferences passed motions condemning what they described as the growing use of temporary workers and employers' strategies of substituting temporary for permanent workers. Yet at the same time local officers and shop stewards of the same unions were finding themselves party to local, enterprise-level agreements setting the terms

143

under which temporary workers could for the first time be used, or under which their use could be expanded. Most regarded the special circumstances in which the enterprises concerned found themselves a legitimate reason for consenting. There was probably no (easy) alternative to the use of temporary workers; and if they were to be employed, at least such workers should otherwise have the same rights as regular workers. Many local officers and shop stewards confessed to a bad conscience about seeing temporary workers coming in and then going out again to unemployment. Some admitted that the creation of a 'buffer group' of temporary workers actually enhanced the employment security of their 'core' members; indeed, some 'temporary worker agreements' were also 'no redundancy agreements' for the bulk for the workforce [see Chapter 7].

Nevertheless, such national-local contradictions could not be sustained for long. Several unions, conscious that their membership had fallen in recent years and looking round for new areas of recruitment, homed in on 'non-standard' workers. The General and Municipal union concentrated on casuals, seasonals and fixed-term contract workers, on part-timers and even on the self-employed; the Transport and General union on the same categories of temporary worker, on part-timers, and even on agency workers. Special recruitment drives have been organised, 'model agreements' governing when and under what conditions temporary workers might be used, and 'casual workers' charters' have been drawn up. Some unions, notably the electricians, have gone further, establishing local registers of (otherwise) unemployed members from which employers have to draw when filling the temporary positions enterprise level agreements have permitted them to create.

Whilst the unions' attempts to regulate the use of the 'new' temporary workers might prove successful, their attempts to organise 'traditional' temporary workers seem much less likely to bear fruit. It is not only that in the past unions have not tried or wanted to recruit such workers; temporary workers themselves have often had no real interest in being recruited. The attachment to work of many of them is rather marginal - itself intimately related to the fact that frequently their temporary jobs are also part-time jobs [see Chapter 2]. Agency workers, operating in sectors of acute labour shortage, usually feel themselves adequately rewarded by the workings of the market and do not feel the need to have any institution intervening on their behalf. Trade unions will face an uphill struggle to convince seasonal and casual workers of the benefits of membership. If they stand a chance at all of appealing to agency workers, it will only be (as the General and Municipal union have done in trying to attract the self-employed) by appealing to individualist, entrepreneurial interests rather than collectivist, employee interests.

Temporary working over time

An important aim of the study was to see if there had been any growth in the use of temporary working in Britain in recent years. There has been much discussion of attempts to increase labour force 'flexibility' and the rise of the 'flexible firm', although it is not always clear if this discussion is based upon descriptions, predictions or prescriptions. One element of 'flexibility' is 'numerical flexibility' and temporary workers provide an important means of achieving 'numerical flexibility'.

Consistent data on the extent of temporary working are not available over time: the results from the mid-1970s worker-directed survey are in no way comparable with those of the 1984 employer-directed survey and also cannot really be compared to those of the LFS. The LFS itself has asked a consistent question about temporary working only since 1983. Moreover, before its results can be used, participants in special employment measures have to be excluded. As we have aleady seen, these make up a sizeable number of temporary workers and in the years since 1983 there has been a major expansion of special employment measures in Britain. When participants in the latter are purged from the statistics we find no real growth in the period 1983 to 1986. In 1983 temporary workers not in special schemes made up 5.5 per cent of the total labour force not in special schemes; in 1986 they made up 5.6 per cent [see Table 1.13].

The more limited information on employers' use of temporary workers available from WIRS provides further evidence of the absence of any significant change. The 1980 WIRS contained an identical question on the use of fixed-term contract workers as did the 1984 survey (the question on the use of agency workers was not consistent). We reported

145

earlier that in 1984 20 per cent of all establishments used such workers and seven per cent used them in numbers equal to at least five per cent of their labour forces. In 1980 the respective proportions were 19 per cent and seven per cent [see Table 3.3].

Finally, the discussion of the 'flexible firm' and of the 'new' use of temporary workers centres on the manufacturing sector. Our fieldwork brought us into contact with a number of organisations in that sector which could be described as 'new' users, seeking to manage a climate of increased 'uncertainty'. Whilst they provided material for a case study, our impression was that these organisations were exceptions - firms facing particular problems. Indeed, in the course of our research it became increasingly clear that many of those commenting upon the 'new' temporary working were making reference to the same small number of examples of this practice - examples, moreover, in which the number of temporary workers actually employed was often very low [see Chapter 7].

Conclusions

In many analyses of the labour markets, temporary working is referred to not only as a 'non-standard' form of employment but also as a 'precarious' and a 'new' form of employment. Indeed, for some commentators the three adjectives appear to be almost synonyms. On the basis of the research we undertook, we are doubtful whether either of the latter two epithets are generally appropriate. As we said earlier, labour law does not, in general, give a lower degree of protection to temporary workers *qua* temporary workers. Consequently some long-service temporary workers enjoy the full range of statutory employment rights, but other short-service permanent workers enjoy none of them. Equally, there are temporary workers who, because they are deemed in labour law to be self-employed, enjoy no statutory employment rights. Some of these, however, enjoy a high degree of de facto employment security because they operate in tight occupational/regional labour markets. Among those who do not, many are not interested in building up the sort of long-term relationship characterised by mutual obligations which a system built upon rights implies; some are 'voluntary' temporary workers only wanting occasional work, others are 'involuntary' ones regarding their current job as, at best, 'stop-gap' employment.

Employers' reasons for using temporary workers are largely traditional ones. There are examples of a 'new' use of temporary workers, but at present these remain the exception rather than the rule. Neither of the two sets of consistent time series data which exist indicate a significant increase in recourse to temporary workers. Since one of these - the LFS - spans a period of economic growth, and since it is argued that the demand for temporary workers grows faster than demand for labour as a whole in periods of rising economic activity, this finding is particularly striking. It would certainly be unwise to argue that in this respect there has been any fundamental change in personnel practices in recent years.

What might, however, be the case is that a greater proportion of people in temporary jobs are 'involuntary' rather than 'voluntary' temporary workers than a decade or so ago, in other words that the structure of the temporary worker population has changed over time. Cross-sectional data showing a strong relationship between the share of temporary working which is 'involuntary' and the level of unemployment in a region [see Chapter 4] suggests that 'involuntary' temporary workers might have increasingly displaced 'voluntary' ones, at least in certain occupations and industries. Equally, there are some indications [see Chapter 7] that the temporary workers employed by 'new' users of temporary labour are more likely to be 'involuntary' temporary workers than those employed by 'traditional' users. This is an important question, one which we were not able to pursue in our research as far as we would have liked. It certainly merits further examination.

References

Atkinson J., *Flexibility, Uncertainty and Manpower Management.* Institute of Manpower Studies (Report. No. 89), University of Sussex, 1984.

Bowers, J., D. Deaton and J. Turk, *Labour Hoarding in British Industry.* Basil Blackwell, Oxford, 1982.

Carey, M. and K. Hazelbaker, 'Employment growth in the temporary help industry', in *Monthly Labour Review*, Vol. 109, No. 4 (April 1986), pp 37-44.

CBI, *Twenty-five years of 'ups' and 'downs'.* Confederation of British Industry, London, 1983.

Clifton, R. and C. Tatton Brown, *Impact of employment legislation on small firms.* Department of Employment (Research Paper No. 6), July 1979.

Connor H., and R. Pearson, *Information Technology Manpower into the 1990s.* Institute of Manpower Studies, University of Sussex, April 1986.

Creigh, S. et al, Self-employment in Britain: Results from the Labour Force Surveys 1981-1984, in *Employment Gazette*, June, 1986, pp 183-194.

Cunningham, J., 'Temps to Soar, says forecast', in *The Guardian*, 28/7/87.

Daniel, W., *The Unemployed Flow: Stage 1 Interim Report.* Policy Studies Institute, (Research Paper No. 81.1), London, 1981.

Daniel W. and N. Millward, *Workplace Industrial Relations in Britain.* Gower, Aldershot, 1983.

Daniel, W. and E. Stilgoe, *The Impact of Employment Protection Laws.* Policy Studies Institute (Report. No. 577), London, 1978.

Davies, P. and M. Freedland, *Labour Law: Texts and Materials* (2nd edn.). Weidenfeld and Nicolson, London, 1984.

Deakin, S., 'Labour law and the developing employment relationship in the UK', in *Cambridge Journal of Economics*, Vol. 10 (1986), pp 225-246.

Evans, S., J. Goodman and L. Hargreaves, *Unfair dismissal law and employment practice in the 1980s.* Department of Employment (Research Paper No. 53), London, July 1985.

FPS, Evidence of the Federation of Personnel Services, in House of Lords Select Committee on the European Communities, Session 1982-1983, 6th Report, *Temporary Work: Proposal for a Directive Concerning Temporary Work.* London, HMSO (HLP (82-83) 65), 1983.

Greer, D. and S. Rhoades, A test of the reserve labour hypothesis, in *Economic Journal*, Vol. 87 (1977), pp 290-299.

Hakim, C., *Employers' use of outwork: A study using the 1980 Workplace Industrial Relations Survey and the 1981 National Survey of Homeworking.* Department of Employment (Research Paper No. 44), London, 1984.

Hakim, C., 'Homeworking in Britain: Key findings from the national survey of home-based workers', in *Employment Gazette*, Feb. 1987, pp 92-104.

Hansard, 'Seasonal Workers (Definition)' (Adjournment Debate, 4/2/87), in House of Commons *Hansard*, Vol. 109, Issue No. 1405, col.1116-1122.

IDS, *Redundancy. Incomes Data Services* (Employment Law Handbook No. 24), London, Dec. 1982.

IDS, *Part-timers, temps and job sharers.* Incomes Data Services (Employment Law Handbook No. 31), London, April, 1985.

IDS, *Fixed-term and temporary contracts (Parts 1 and 2)*, in Incomes Data Services Brief No. 332, pp 7-10 and No. 334, pp 7-10, September and October 1986(a).

IDS, *Keyboard Staff's Pay.* Incomes Data Services Study No. 368, Aug. 1986(b).

IDS, *Computer Staff Pay.* Incomes Data Services Study No. 354, Jan. 1986(c).

IRS, 'Casual wine waiter is an employee', in *Industrial Relations Legal Information Bulletin*, No. 292, Nov. 1985(a), pp 10-11.

IRS, 'Mathematical approach to temporary cessation wrong', in *Industrial Relations Legal Information Bulletin*, No. 292, Nov. 1985(b), pp 11-12.

IRS, 'Using temporary and sub-contract labour', in *Industrial Relations Review and Report*, No. 365, April 1986(a), pp 2-7.

IRS, 'CSEU takes temporary workers on board', in *Industrial Relations Review and Report*, No. 372, July 1986(b), pp 11-12.

IRS, Temporary workers register agreed in Excel's strike free deal, in *Industrial Relations Review and Report*, No. 381, Dec 1986(c), pp 6-10.

IRS, 'Trade unions and temporary workers', in *Industrial Relations Review and Report*, No. 391, May 1987, pp 12-15.

Isaac, D., 'Where Manpower mops up', in *Management Today*, April 1985, pp 86-90.

Joray, P., 'United States', in *Cahier* No. 20. International Institute of Temporary Work, Den Haag, 1981, pp 291-306.

Key Note, *Report on Employment Agencies.* Key Note Publications Ltd., London, 1985.

Leighton, P., Case Note on 'O'Kelly v. Trust House Forte PLC', in *Industrial Law Journal*, Vol. 13 (1984), pp 62-66.

Leighton, P., Case Note on 'Wickens v. Champion Employment', in *Industrial Law Journal*, Vol.14 (1985), pp 54-57.

Leighton, P., *Marginal Workers, in R. Lewis (ed), Labour Law in Britain*. Basil Blackwell, Oxford, 1986, pp. 503-527.

LRD, *Temporary Workers - a negotiators' guide*. Labour Research Department, London, 1987.

Magnum, G., D. Mayall and K. Nelson. 'The temporary help industry: A response to the dual internal labour market' in *Industrial and Labour Relations Review*, Vol. 38 (1985), pp 599-613.

Manpower, *Corporate Profile - 1985/6*. The Manpower Group of Companies, Slough, 1985.

Manpower, *A Survey of Temporary and Permanent Office Staff June/July 1986, Summary tables*. The Manpower Group of Companies, Slough, 1986.

Martin, J. and B. Butcher, The quality of proxy information - some results from a large scale study, in *The Statistician*, Vol. 31 (1982), pp 293-319.

Meager, N. *Temporary Work in Great Britain: its growth and changing rationales*. Institute of Manpower Studies (Report. No. 106), University of Sussex, 1985.

Millward, N. and M. Stevens, *British Workplace Industrial Relations 1980-1984*. Gower, Aldershot, 1986.

Moylan, S., J. Millar and R. Davies, *For Richer, for Poorer?* DHSS Cohort Study of Unemployed Men. Department of Health and Social Security (Research Report. No. 11), HMSO, London, 1984.

MSC, Temporary Work in Great Britain, in *MSC Labour Market Quarterly Report*, Nov. 1985, pp 7-9.

NCC, *NCC Members Survey 1985*. The National Computing Centre, Manchester, 1985.

Newton, S. and S. Parker, 'Who are the temporary workers?', in *Department of Employment Gazette*, June 1975, pp 507-511.

Nickell, S., 'The Determinants of Equilibrium Unemployment in Britain', in *Economic Journal*, Vol. 92 (1982), pp 555-575.

NUT, *1983 NUT Survey on the Use of Fixed-Term Contracts*. National Union of Teachers, London, Sept. 1983.

OECD, 'Moving in and out of unemployment: the incidence and patterns of recurrent unemployment in selected OECD countries, in OECD *Employment Outlook*, Sept. 1985, pp 99-114.

Parker, S. and A. Sirker, *Temporary Workers: A report of an enquiry carried out for the Employment Service Agency*. Office of Population Censuses and Surveys, London, 1976.

Phelps Brown, E., *Report of the Committee of Inquiry under Prof. E. H. Phelps Brown into Certain Matters concerning Labour in Building and Civil Engineering*. Cmnd. 3714, HMSO, London, 1968.

Piore, M., 'Perspectives on labour market flexibility', in *Industrial Relations: a journal of economy and society*, Vol. 25 (1986), pp 146-166.

Reed, *Reed Employment 'Temp'Ting Survey*. Reed Employment, London, April 1986.

Rothwell S. and P. Mingard, *Comparative Labour Costs of Employing Permanent Staff and Using Temporary Workers Through Agencies*. The Centre for Employment Policy Studies, Henley, 1985.

Secretary of State for Employment, *Building Businesses ..... Not Barriers*. Cmnd. 9794, HMSO, London, May 1986.

Smith, R. and M. Rowland, *Rights Guide to Non Means-Tested Social Security Benefits* (9th edn.). Child Poverty Action Group, London, 1986.

Stern, J., 'Job durations of men becoming unemployed', in *British Journal of Industrial Relations*. Vol. XX (1982), pp 373-376.

Syrett, M., *Temporary Work Today*. Federation of Recruitment and Employment Services Ltd., London, 1985.

Towers, B, and M. Harrison, 'Great Britain: Developments in the British Temporary Work Market' in *Cahier* No. 20. International Institute of Temporary Work, Den Haag, 1981, pp 275-282.

Turner, P., 'After the Community Programme - results of the first follow-up survey', in *Employment Gazette*, Jan 1985, pp 9-14.

Wilson, D., *Dockers: the impact of industrial change.* Fontana, London, 1972.

Wood, D., *Men registering as unemployed in 1978: A longitudinal study.* Department of Health and Social Security (DHSS Cohort Study of Unemployed Men Working Paper No. 1), London, 1982.